Learning Services

Please return
on or before
the last date
stamped below

CITY COLLEGE
NORWICH

2 4 MAY 2011

2 2 MAY 2012

208 532

Lucas Rosenblatt   Judith Meyer
Edith Beckmann

Cooking with Coffee

60 recipes using Fair Trade coffee

 Fair Trade Cookbooks

© 2003
New Internationalist Publications™ Ltd
55 Rectory Road
Oxford OX4 1BW, UK
www.newint.org

New Internationalist is a registered trade mark

Cover design: Dora Eichenberger-Hirter, Birrwil
Text design: Ursula Mötteli, Grafikdesign, Aarau
Photos: Andreas Thumm, Freiburg im Breisgau
(all the recipe illustrations)
Robert Schmid, Obererlinsbach:
(Pages 2, 4/5, 6/7, 11, 16, 19, 22/23, 27, 29,
32, 33, 136, 138/9
Procafé Bern:
(Pages 15, 18, 24, 25, 26, 28, 31, 34, 36, 37, 38)
Helvetas, Zürich: (Pages 8/9)
Lithos: Neue Schwitter AG, Allschwil
English language version editor: Troth Wells
English language translation produced by
Translate-A-Book, Oxford
Printing and binding: Amadeus
Printed in Italy by Amadeus

This book was first published in 2002 by
EDITION FONA GmbH
CH-5600 Lenzburg - www.fona.ch
The book appeared simultaneously in French by
Edition VIRIDIS, CH-2800 Delément

Acknowledgement
Many thanks to Globus in Lucerne for providing
the crockery for the recipe photos

ISBN 1 904456 07 3

Contents

DESSERTS

BAKING

All recipes serve 4 unless otherwise stated.

THE STORY OF COFFEE

A Bean Conquers the World

This fragrant beverage has a history as dark as itself. Eastern storytellers have handed down legends of its origins through the generations. One tale tells of a goatherd called Chalid. Playing the flute as he went, he wandered with his goats through the mountain forests of Abyssinia, present-day Ethiopia. As dusk fell over the land he would summon his flock with a few musical trills and then drive them home into the village. However, one evening his flute-playing was in vain and he had to go to look for his goats.

The truants had gathered round some bushes with rich green leaves and red berries and were behaving very strangely. They leapt in the air, bleated joyfully and would not go home with their shepherd. Chalid thought the animals were bewitched and was terrified of his father's anger.

Next day the goats hurried back to the bushes with the red berries and their jasmine-scented blossoms. Becoming curious, the boy nibbled at some leaves. They tasted bitter, but as he was chewing them he felt a little tingle on his tongue, which spread pleasantly throughout his whole body.

Stimulant from the Magic Bush

Then Chalid nibbled at the berries as well. They tasted mild and sweet. The seeds were immersed in a thick, tasty juice. As he bit into them he had the feeling that he would never be tired or grumpy again.

In the evening Chalid told his father about the magic bushes. In next to no time the news spread from village to village. The inhabitants of the old kingdom of Kaffa began to make an infusion from the leaves and berries. They called the stimulating drink *qahwa*, which became 'coffee'. Although the spelling varies, this is the word now used in most languages of the world.

The first time coffee was mentioned in writing was in the 10th century by the Arabic doctor Rhazes. However, it is likely that the bushes had already been cultivated for centuries before that. It is said that the prophet Muhammad (570-632 AD), the founder of Islam, was already an enthusiastic *qahwa* drinker, as it kept him awake for his night prayers. The resourceful Abyssinians soon developed tastier ways of accessing the stimulating caffeine than simply infusing the leaves and berries in hot water. They pounded the beans with a mortar and pestle and mixed them with animal fat. They made wine from the fermented berries, which they also called *qahwa*.

A Pilgrims' Tonic

A drink that makes people euphoric but not inebriated inevitably attracts a large following. Later, the beans were roasted and ground and then water was poured on the powder. Coffee houses, called *Kaveh kane*, were established. The first was in Makkah (Mecca), Muhammad's birth place, the most important place of pilgrimage and therefore also of flourishing trade.

Coffee houses spread rapidly as a result of the growing popularity of the black beverage, enjoyed sociably in sweet idleness. Coffee drove away sleep and tiredness, so all night long Arabs could indulge their great gifts of storytelling and poetry.

One day the Governor of Makkah, Khair-Beg, learned that mocking verses were circulating about him and his ambitious reform plans. His researches revealed that the coffee drinkers were the culprits. Immediately, in the year 1511, he forcibly shut down all the coffee houses in Makkah. However, when the Sultan of Egypt, himself an enthusiastic coffee drinker, heard about it, the Governor cancelled this decree.

Turkish Coffee

For nearly a century the flourishing coffee trade remained firmly in Turkish hands. Between 1516 and 1518, Selim I (1467-1520), Sultan of Constantinople, conquered Syria, Palestine, Yemen and Egypt. These conquered countries became the Ottoman Empire. He had mainly financed his conquests through the coffee trade. Muslim pilgrims took care of the necessary 'publicity' for the drink as they traveled from far away countries, not only to Makkah, but also to Medina, the site of Muhammad's tomb.

The Turks shipped the precious beans mainly to the Yemeni port of Mocha; hence the term 'Mocha' for coffee. The cargo reached Suez via the sea route through the Red Sea. From there camel caravans brought it to the warehouses of Alexandria, the old capital of Egypt. In the Mediterranean port a vigorous trade grew up with Venetian and French traders.

The Turks kept a strict watch over their lucrative business and defended their monopoly – not a single ripe coffee berry was allowed to leave the country. Eventually the Muslim pilgrim Baba Budan succeeded in smuggling some seeds out. He took them with him to south India and cultivated a few plantations in the Mysore mountains.

In 1616 the Dutch, who dominated worldwide sea trading routes at that time, managed to steal a bush in Aden. They shipped it to Holland and with its fruit they founded Dutch coffee cultivation in Ceylon, the modern Sri Lanka. From there Hendrik Zwaardekroon took a few bushes to Java (in Indonesia) in 1699. Cultivation followed in Sumatra, Timor, Bali and other East Indian islands. Trade in the modest little beans flourished because prosperous Europeans discovered their passion for the sinfully expensive dark drink.

> 'When you go to your wife, keep yourself free from worries and be cheerful.
> You should not have eaten too much, but could well have drunk a strengthening coffee.'
>
> Sheikh Nafsawi, 1516

Victory March through Europe

In 1554 Hakim and Schems, coffee traders from the Syrian cities of Aleppo and Damascus, opened the first coffee house on European soil in Constantinople, ancient Byzantium, the present-day Istanbul. The flourishing trading city on the Bosphorus, the seaway between the two continents of Europe and Asia, was a popular destination for traders, scholars and adventurers.

'Among other things, you have a good drink, which is black as ink and helpful for afflictions, especially of the stomach,' wrote the Augsburg doctor Leonhard Rauwolf in his account of his travels in 1582. The Italian physician and botanist Prosper Alpinus has given us the first detailed drawings and descriptions of the coffee plant. He handed these on in his book *De Plantis Aegypti Liber*, published in Venice in 1592.

From this city built on a lagoon, which was then the most important European port for commerce, the cheery coffee bean from the East conquered half of Italy. A dispute promptly arose about the Muslim drink. Pope Clement VIII, who died in 1605, thought about banning this 'Satan's brew'. However, the wise head of the Church in the end pronounced a judgment of Solomon:

'It would be a sin to leave such a delicious drink to unbelievers. Let us defeat the devil by blessing him for having given us a truly Christian drink!'

The businesslike Venetians did not need to be told twice and bought in whole shiploads of coffee, which now came with the Pope's blessing. In 1645 the first coffee house in the Christian West opened its doors in St Mark's Square. Even the lemonade sellers, who also sold cocoa and alcohol in the streets of Venice, became involved in the lucrative coffee business.

A Rising Tide

In the second half of the 17th century the coffee wave flooded the whole of Europe at what was a breakneck speed for those times, when travel was so difficult. In 1650 the first coffee house on British soil opened in Oxford and two years later another was set up in London. In 1559 the French port of Marseilles hosted France's first one; the Dutch in The Hague and Amsterdam had theirs four years later. In 1672 a stylish establishment opened its doors in Paris. On German soil, the first one started up in 1673 in Bremen and four years later another opened in Hamburg. It was not only the drink from the East that was new, but also the serving of it in public places, which became bustling meeting points for business partners and traders.

The Viennese with their famous coffee-house culture first had to inflict a crushing defeat on the Turks. The Polish-born Georg Frantzen Kolschitzky made an important contribution to the victory in 1683. Wearing a turban and pantaloons, he and his servant Michaelowitz outwitted the enemy besiegers. They achieved the almost unbelievable feat of smuggling a letter out of the starving city of Vienna to their allies, appealing for reinforcements.

While the Polish army encountered fierce resistance, the Duke of Lorraine's troops, in a surprise flank attack, managed to force the Ottomans to flee on 12 September 1683. The Turks had to leave most of their possessions behind. Among these, several hundred sacks of coffee were found, which the brave Kolschitzky claimed for his courageous services as a messenger. He bamboozled the authorities once more because they thought the pale brown beans were worthless animal fodder.

White Coffee for the European Palate

The canny Kolschitzky experimented assiduously to adapt the roasted beans to Viennese tastes. His travels in the East had made him familiar with the Turkish drink and how to prepare it. Without more ado he strained out the coffee grounds, which were traditionally left in the hot brew. Then he added sugar syrup and milk.

Soon the busy Viennese coffee houses provided newspapers for their customers to read. And in order to mock and humiliate the defeated Turks – whose weapons bore a crescent moon on them – the *kipferl* was created, a crisp, semi-circular puff-pastry roll, which was later transformed into the French croissant.

Vienna's first Coffee House
(Oil painting by Franz Scham, 1823-83; property of Dr Julius Meini, Vienna)

Coffee Culture

Coffee and the places where it is served have left a deep impression on the history of Europe. Whereas wine and beer – the latter even drunk for breakfast – tend to befuddle the mind, coffee sharpens it. In the 17th century nutritious beer was more or less a liquid bread. An average English family – including children and the elderly – would consume a respectable 3 quarts/3 liters/5^1/$_4$ pints per head per day. Shakespeare's notorious Falstaff sends his regards...

No wonder the sobering Turkish drink became the fuel of intellectual life. Towards the end of the 17th and throughout the 18th century the coffee houses of Europe became centers of communication, trading and information exchange, and also hotbeds of rumor-mongering. The politically involved and agitators found a welcoming audience there.

In addition, seditious newspapers, which in those days were often hand-written rather than printed, circulated in the coffee houses. By 1700 there were more than 2,000 such dens in London alone. The newspapers were so popular that the coffee houses also acted as editorial offices. This is later documented by Richard Steele, editor of the weekly *Tatler*, which at the beginning of the 18th century gave The Grecian coffee house as its editorial address.

A Classless Society

London's coffee houses were then known as 'penny universities' because that was the price of a cup of coffee, inclusive of stimulating conversation. What was revolutionary for the British way of life was that no class differences existed here. Customers all sat at the same table, regardless of their profession or where they came from.

Anyone who could pay was welcome and many of the frequent visitors were business people. Coffee houses took over the role of company offices. Lloyd's Coffee House, founded by Edward Lloyd in 1688, was a meeting place for all who had business with trade and shipping. Towards the end of the 18th century Lloyds Insurance Company arose from it, which still operates worldwide today.

The British coffee clique excluded women and children until 1730. They were left with tea shops where, among other things, they lambasted the gentlemen's clubs.

The women's movement expressed its outrage that men preferred to sit in coffee houses instead of taking care of their families and earning a living, with a robust pamphlet that

Vienna's coffee house culture is known and loved far beyond Austria.

appeared in 1674, *Women's Petition against Coffee*. In it the angry women accused their husbands of impotence because coffee was turning them into eunuchs. On 29 December 1675, King Charles II (1630-85) issued a proclamation closing the coffee houses. They were, he claimed, refuges for idleness in which false, malicious and scandalous rumors were let loose upon a world that took it upon itself to denigrate His Majesty's rule and disturb the peace. However, the King had made this decision without taking his subjects into account. The fury and dismay were so great that he feared the monarchy would be overthrown. On 8 January 1676, two days before the ban on coffee houses was to come into force, the King grudgingly withdrew his decree.

Breeding Grounds for Rebellion

Coffee also wrote history in France. In 1669 the Turkish Ambassador, Soliman Aga, introduced the new-fangled drink to the French court with much pomp and ceremony and in the face of energetic protest by Liselotte von der Pfalz (1652-1722), sister-in-law to Louis XIV, the Sun King. The 'soot-colored water' did nothing for the determined beer drinker; wine producers opposed it because they saw coffee as a serious rival.

The internet café is a popular meeting place, especially for young people.

But reformers, rebels and writers adopted this alcohol-free drink as a cause. Reformers waged a fierce war against alcohol, which makes people unsteady, blunts their sensibilities and leaves them incapable of thinking clearly. Spirits, wine and beer did not suit this period of enlightened humanism in which the individual was central and self-reliant.

The French Revolution, which led to the storming of the Bastille (the Paris fortress and symbol of tyranny) on 14 July 1789, had its origin in night-long discussions – thanks to the stimulation of coffee. The French Court's irrepressible love of extravagance had brought the people to the edge of ruin and created a serious famine.

The French historian Jules Michelet (1798-1874) maintained that coffee had abruptly revealed the reality of things with a lightning flash of truth. In the cavern of the Café Procope in Paris the assembled company glimpsed the light of revolution by means of the black drink.

The French novelist Honoré de Balzac (1799-1850) was just as keen on caffeine. He wrote like one possessed, with a steaming coffee pot always beside him. For *café au lait*, his fellow citizens' milky coffee, he could spare only a weary smile. The eloquent Balzac, who left 90 books about French society, consumed finely powdered roasted coffee with a little hot water, unstrained and black as night. 'My brain needs this stimulus, even if it is dangerous... I have horrible stomach pains,' he wrote in 1845. Coffee was the driving force of his genius. Balzac feelingly described the reason for his excessive coffee consumption in these words: 'After the first cups the characters stand up, ink covers the paper, because the waking condition has begun and ends with torrents of black water, so that at the end of the battle all that remains is black powder...'

Opposition and *Coffee Cantata*

By the middle of the 17th century the fashion for coffee swept into Switzerland. In Neuenburg and Geneva the hot drink soon met with upper-class approval, but in Basle coffee encountered strong opposition. In 1769 the authorities of this city on the Rhine, where three countries meet, banned the 'health-destroying evil' with the threat of a hefty fine of 'five pounds'. However, they did not want to spoil things for tourists who were bringing prosperity to the region, so innkeepers were excepted from the ban and permitted to offer coffee to travelers. The city fathers clearly were not at all worried about the health of visitors. In 1722 the puritanical Zürich Council prohibited the serving of coffee not only at guild dinners but also at public festivals.

Although by the second half of the 17th century the precious beans from the Yemeni port of Mocha had already been shipped to Bremen and Hamburg, the Turkish drink had a hard time of it with Teutonic beer drinkers. The German coffee houses did not begin to compare with the literary circles of London and Paris. However the Zimmermann coffee house in Leipzig did achieve fame. Johann Sebastian Bach was the organist at Leipzig's St Thomas's Church from 1723-50. With his *Collegium Musicum* he played in the Zimmermann coffee house. Bach's four suites for orchestra were performed there, as well as his humorous *Coffee Cantata*.

> 'Father, don't be so unkind!
> If I can't drink my cup of coffee three times a day I'll become a straggly goat, to my great dismay.
> Oh! how sweet the coffee's taste is, sweeter than a thousand kisses, smoother far than Muscat wine.
> Coffee, coffee, give me mine, and if someone wants to treat me let them offer me a coffee.'

> From the *Coffee Cantata*, 1732, Johann Sebastian Bach

Classic Colonial Product

With growing popularity and increasing demand, coffee lost its innocence. Trade in the beans was extremely lucrative. They became a classic colonial product, with all the accompanying sinister features. The people of producer countries had no real choice other than to cultivate coffee at the behest of their feudal masters for a miserable reward.

Even worse, the land belonging to the indigenous people was ruthlessly annexed so that they did not even have enough to grow their own vegetables. The most brutal measures were used to make the rebellious see reason. Uprisings were bloodily suppressed. Where local people, for example in the Caribbean islands and South America, withdrew in resignation to infertile mountain regions, their colonial masters brought in slaves. Trade in human beings reached incredible levels. In Brazil alone, in 1828 more than a million slaves were at work, corresponding to nearly a third of the whole population.

Slavery

Where coffee flourishes, power, politics, repression and exploitation also enter the picture. East Timor only recently became independent, on 20 May 2002. Between 1586 and 1975 the Portuguese controlled this country, which belongs to the small Sunda Islands. The Dutch had installed themselves in the west of the island and by 1700 they had already planted coffee.

Coffee traditionally has been East Timor's most important export. The climatic conditions, with a top daytime temperature of 30°C/86°F dropping at night to no lower than 24°C/75°F, as well as plenty of rainfall, are ideal for cultivating coffee. This profitable raw material was one of the reasons why Indonesia occupied East Timor in December 1975 after the withdrawal of the Portuguese.

Coffee cultivation has also been an important factor in the conflict between the Singhalese and Tamils in Sri Lanka, formerly Ceylon. The first plantations were set up towards the end of the 17th century under Dutch control. When the British took over from the Dutch in 1825 they intensified coffee cultivation. The island's highlands bloomed with thousands of coffee bushes. Between 1812 and 1845 production rose one-hundred-fold, from 152 to 15,200 tons of raw coffee. There was a shortage of labor, mainly because the Singhalese farmers refused to toil on the plantations as ill-paid day laborers. 'So planters are instructed to use

coolies from the Malabar Coast (Tamils from south India) as manpower,' states a document from the 19th century. Even today tensions remain between the two groups.

Repression

The Germans began coffee cultivation in Guatemala and Nicaragua in Central America. The first plantations were established in 1868 in the moderate climate of the Alta Verapaz Province in the heart of Guatemala. Within a few years German settlers had driven out the indigenous people and brought most of the coffee production under their own control.

In Guatemala's mountain regions, which are 980-5,000 feet/300-1,500 meters high, they cultivated the valuable Maragogype variety of Arabica coffee, which was particularly highly prized in Germany because of its large beans. About 70 per cent of total production was firmly in German hands. In 1899 about 20,000 tons of raw coffee was exported from Guatemala to Germany.

The Union of Hamburg Coffee Import Agents and Brokers, founded in 1888, became the hub of the European coffee trade. Today this Hanseatic city's turnover is about ten million sacks of raw coffee per year – about one tenth of total world production.

A Stubborn Plant

The coffee plant is a stubborn child of the tropics. It grows all round the globe, although only along the equatorial belt, limited in its range by the reach of the tropical sun. Average annual temperatures of 59-77°F/15-25°C, sufficient rainfall at the right time and altitudes of 2,000-5,900 feet/600-1,800 meters above sea level are ideal for the valuable high-quality Arabica varieties.

Until the middle of the 19th century only the Coffea arabica species of coffee plants were cultivated. However, more than a thousand years of cultivation – with yields constantly being forced up – have seriously impaired this variety. Countless pests and coffee rust (*Hemileia vastatrix*, a devastating fungus) kept destroying large parts of the harvests. With a vastatrix attack the bushes lose their leaves and might even die. The damaging fungus first appeared in 1869 in Ceylon (Sri Lanka). It spread to become an epidemic and destroyed all the plantations on the island.

So the hectic search began for more robust coffee plants. White farmers in the Belgian Congo, the modern Democratic Republic of Congo, struck lucky. They named the beans of the wild-growing coffee bushes (*Coffea canephora*) 'Robusta', because these proved to be disease resistant and fruitful. Robusta coffee grows on lower ground than Arabica and under wetter and warmer conditions. The beans are smaller and rounder. They contain almost double the amount of caffeine as Arabica and have a stronger, harsher and more bitter flavor.

Types of coffee beans:
Robusta (left) and
Arabica (right)

The Growing Plant

The evergreen coffee plant belongs to the madder family (*Rubiaceae*) and so is an aristocratic cousin of the common British woodruff. It grows as a bush or tree, reaching a height of 13-26 feet/4-8 meters. To make picking easier the plants in plantations are usually cut back to a bush height of 5-10 feet/1.5-3 meters. The plant requires deep, humus-rich soil to fix its roots, which are 3-6 feet/1-2 meters long.

Coffee trees and bushes prefer light shade. Traditionally, the seedlings are planted under banana, avocado, papaya and other trees, whose leaves spread out to protect the young coffee shoots, which are scarcely 20 inches/50 cm high. They are kept in the nursery and tended carefully for about a year until they have grown.

The young shoots are kept in bags with a little soil, tended in nurseries and then planted out, so that they can grow into bushes.

It is an amazing sight – all the stages of development from blossom to ripe, dark-red berries on the same branch.

Harvesting and sorting coffee berries

From Flowers to Fruit

Another three or four years' care and nurturing are required until the coffee bush flowers for the first time. Small clusters of blossoms nestle close to the leaves and have a pleasant jasmine-like scent.

From flowering to the ripe fruit takes about six months for Robusta coffee, but almost a year for Arabica, which is grown at higher altitudes.

The coffee berries have a long ripening period and the bushes simultaneously bear flowers and fruit at different stages of ripeness, from green to yellow to a shiny dark red. For high-quality coffee the ripe berries are picked by hand again and again over a period of weeks. A less arduous procedure is strip-picking in which the coffee berries are removed from the branches with a sort of comb. Unfortunately, this harvesting method also removes the green berries, which have to be sorted out by hand afterwards.

A full harvest can take five to seven years. Each bush yields about 1-4 pounds/0.5-2 kilos, corresponding to 3-11 ounces/ 80-320 grams of roasted coffee. Each berry contains two coffee beans, which are embedded in a bitter-sweet pulp. Occasionally a coffee berry contains just one round bean, called a peaberry.

The coffee beans are surrounded by a hard shell, the parchment layer. Under this lies the silver skin. By various expensive processes the pulp, parchment and silver skin have to be removed before the raw coffee is ready for roasting.

Structure of the coffee berry

Coffee bean
Parchment (parchment shell)
Silver skin
Pulp
Red outer skin

The Long Road to Raw Coffee

Because the coffee berry pulp starts to rot shortly after picking, the berries have to be processed as soon as possible. The raw coffee can be prepared either dry or wet.

Dry Preparation

The dry process is mainly used in Brazil and Africa and in other regions where water is scarce. The freshly harvested coffee berries, cleaned of impurities, are spread out on the ground to dry. They are turned frequently to expose them to the sun and to dry them. At night they are piled into heaps and covered, to protect them from damp.

The pulp has thoroughly dried out if the beans rattle in their shells when shaken. This takes from two to three weeks. In areas where the climate is not suitable for this treatment they may be hot-air dried with special equipment.

Next, the dried berries are broken open by machine and detached from their pulp, parchment and, as much as possible, also from the silver skin. Then the raw coffee is sieved and sorted by size. Top-quality beans may be hand sorted.

Wet Preparation

With this technique, the freshly picked coffee berries are rinsed in water to remove impurities. The best-quality berries sink to the bottom while the poorer ones float to the surface. The poorer quality are prepared separately and do not usually reach the international coffee market.

Swollen from washing, the berries are now crushed by being spun in running water. These so-called pulpers remove most of the pulp. Any remaining pulp ferments and radically affects the taste and aroma of the coffee. The fermentation process takes place in tubs and lasts one to two days. Afterwards the beans are washed and then dried in the sun or in hot-air drying equipment. The parchment shell and part of the silver skin is removed in shelling machines.

Wet preparation: coffee berries are either sieved or rinsed to remove leaves, unripe berries, stones, sand and other impurities, but this process has nothing to do with washing the coffee.

The cleaned and sorted coffee berries are put into special machines, called pulpers, where they are crushed and separated from their pulp.

Ready for Export

Traditionally, raw coffee is traded on the market in weight-units of 132 pounds/60 kilos or sometimes 152 pounds/69 kilos. Coffee beans travel by sea all over the world. Coffee is traded on the New York or London stock markets and transnational corporations from the northern hemisphere dictate the rules of the game. The processing they do is very lucrative and they also benefit from state blessing in the form of subsidy and support. For example, the European Union duty on raw coffee is 4 per cent, on roasted it is 12 per cent and for caffeine-free it is 15 per cent.

Fair Trade – a Glimmer of Hope

Various international projects support farmers in the disadvantaged producer countries, so that they can receive fairer payment. They offer self-help assistance, purchase guarantees at reasonable pre-fixed prices and commit themselves to long-term co-operation. Most of these organizations finance themselves through donations and are often also supported by public money. Under the banner of 'fair trade' they also engage in social projects such as school-building and healthcare, environmentally friendly agriculture and the basic requirements for a life of human dignity, like clean drinking water.

Dried beans:
In the shelling machines the parchment shell and part of the silver skin is taken off.

The pulp removed, the coffee is spread out to dry in the fresh air and constantly turned over.

The raw coffee is drawn into the container through a huge pipe.

The Max Havelaar Foundation

Injustice and exploitation have persisted since coffee became commercialized. People constantly try to do something about this problem. One of them was the Dutch civil servant Eduard Douwes Dekker. From the age of 18 he lived as a state employee in the Dutch colony of Java, one of the Indonesian Sunda Islands. He fought against the evil conditions there without success. He left his post in protest because he could no longer stand by and watch the exploitation of the indigenous people on the coffee plantations.

In 1860 the partly autobiographical book *Max Havelaar or the Coffee Auctions of the Dutch Trading Company* was published under the pseudonym Multatuli. In it Dekker criticized the Dutch landowners, who made their fields fertile using the sweat of their laborers, whose own land they had taken from them. These landowners gave their laborers no pay and enriched themselves at the expense of the poor. The novel and its protagonist Max Havelaar became very popular in Holland. When fair-trade organizations were set up in a number of countries they often chose the symbolic name, Max Havelaar.

Roasting Releases the Aroma

Raw coffee has no smell. It acquires its characteristic, tempting aroma only when it is roasted. The precise roasting process requires a great deal of experience and is usually a well-kept secret. However, the basic procedure has remained almost the same since the middle of the 18th century. Merciless competition has arisen in this area. Gigantic roasting establishments with electronically controlled, fully automated equipment are pitted against the few remaining small shops that devotedly roast coffee by hand.

The greenish-brown raw beans are separated according to type into different silos. They are weighed out according to their blend and driven by compressed air through a pipe system directly into the roasting chamber. The coffee beans are then shaken in a rotating drum, so that the heat is evenly distributed.

A gas or electric burner provides the heat. When they are heated to 212°F/100°C the beans turn light yellow, at 302°F/150°C they become light brown. During roasting the beans reach temperatures of 356-428°F/180-220°C, sometimes even higher. In the process they lose water and therefore weight, between 11 and 18 per cent depending on the degree of roasting.

The 'Crack'

The effect of heat produces a strong pressure within the bean, which bursts like popcorn. In this audible popping, known as 'crack' in the trade, the coffee bean increases its volume by about a quarter, sometimes by as much as a half.

During roasting the sugar contained in the bean is caramelized, giving the beans their typical coffee-brown color. The next stage of the process is carefully scrutinized by the roaster. He carries out constant tests because only a few seconds make a difference to the desired degree of roasting.

Lightly roasted coffee beans have a pale surface and retain more acidity than the darker beans, which are mainly used for espresso. With longer roasting and its accompanying darker color, the beans exude aromatic oils which are deposited on their outer surface, giving them a fine sheen. When they are ground some of this oil is also deposited in the grinder. This has to be cleaned regularly because over time the deposit becomes rancid and can be detrimental to the coffee's taste.

A Fleeting Aroma

Roasting the beans takes 8-15 minutes. As soon as the desired degree of roasting is reached, the beans fall into a rotating sieve to be cooled in a cold air current. They are then usually sprinkled with water. The roasted coffee is commonly prepared for dispatch automatically. The packaging foil is cut and formed into a bag in a single process. The ground coffee or coffee beans are weighed and poured into the bag, which is then sealed. The airtight pack protects the coffee from aroma-loss, light and damp.

The fresher the roast, the better the aroma and therefore the more delicious the flavor of the coffee. In other words, freshly-roasted coffee is designed for immediate use. Once the sealed foil pack is opened the contents should be put into a tightly-closing can and stored in a cool place.

Vacuum-packed coffee, either ground or whole beans, is best for storage. Temperatures above 68°F/20°C adversely affect its quality: you can store coffee beans in their original sealed packets in the freezer, where they will keep fresh for a long time.

Before the raw coffee is stored the roaster does a spot check.

The blends are stored briefly in small 'waiting silos'. The roaster can then adapt the quantity to be roasted quickly and flexibly to the needs of the day.

Section of an air-cleaning and heat-recovery installation. The coffee's fine aroma is sealed in and never reaches the nose.

Unlike in large modern roasting plants, here we can clearly see how the roasted coffee is shaken out of the roasting drum into the cooling sieve. The rotary arms mix up the hot beans and speed up the cooling process.

Traditional test-roast

Filling the coffee bags

Different Types of Coffee

Some people drink coffee precisely because of its stimulating, enlivening effect, while others are kept awake by it. The reason is that coffee beans contain caffeine, a vegetable alkaloid that was discovered in 1820 by the German chemist Friedlieb Ferdinand Runge (1795-1867). He analyzed a few coffee beans given to him by the poet Johann Wolfgang von Goethe (1749-1832).

The caffeine content varies according to the type of coffee. Robusta contains 1.4-3 per cent caffeine, corresponding to about 0.005 ounces/150 mg per cup; Arabica contains 0.8-1.8 per cent, about 0.002 ounces/60 mg per cup. Caffeine is also responsible for about a third of coffee's bitter taste.

Consumed in moderation, caffeine has a positive effect on the nervous system and speeds up heart rate, metabolism and breathing. Blood pressure and body temperature go up. As caffeine produces a slight widening of the blood vessels in the brain, an espresso is helpful for some headaches or a cup of strong coffee is good for poor circulation. Caffeine – also present in black tea, cocoa, maté tea and kola nuts – increases mental activity and dispels tiredness. It stimulates the digestion and acts as a diuretic.

Sufferers from stomach or kidney complaints, high blood pressure or problems with the liver or gall bladder should avoid it, limit their intake or replace it with caffeine-free or low-irritant coffee.

Coffee without Caffeine

Decaffeinated coffee is usually made from Arabica beans because they contain less caffeine naturally. The alkaloid is extracted using steam and solvents. Ludwig Roselius discovered the process in 1905. Since then, techniques for extraction have been refined to preserve better quality. Nevertheless, despite these technological advances, the principle has remained the same.

The raw coffee is treated with steam in rotating drums. This breaks down the caffeine salts and the caffeine can then diffuse through the pores on the surface of the bean. Using solvents such as methylene chloride or ethyl acetate, the caffeine is removed and finally the raw coffee is dried and roasted.

Low-irritant Coffee

People who are sensitive to coffee may still enjoy a cup, but after drinking it may experience heartburn, a burning sensation in the esophagus and the stomach. This is usually caused by irritants that originate when the coffee is roasted and are mainly found in the thin layer of wax covering the coffee beans. Roasted beans also contain tannic and other acids, which intensify under the influence of heat. So coffee should never be warmed up or kept warm for longer than 30 minutes.

In mild, low-irritant coffee part of the wax layer is removed with solvents and then the raw coffee is treated with steam.

Instant Coffee

It takes about 5 pounds/2.3 kilos of raw coffee to produce 2 pounds/1 kilo of soluble coffee powder. This helps to explain the higher price that people pay for this quick and easy method of preparation.

The first stage of the process is the industrial production of a kind of super-strong espresso. Hot water is poured over coarsely ground raw coffee under high pressure and at high temperature. This results in coffee with almost double the concentration of ordinary domestic preparation. There are two different processes that can then be used to remove the water.

With spray-drying, the coffee-concentrate is sprayed into a drying tower and finely atomized. The particles are dried in a hot air stream, with ventilators to suck out the water. This forms tiny coffee grains, which are caught on the base of the spray tower.

With freeze drying, a gentler treatment, the coffee infusion is frozen. The 'coffee ice' is then ground to the desired granule size. The frozen water is steamed off with high-vacuum equipment, leaving behind the freeze-dried coffee granules.

As part of the aromatic substance is lost during the extraction and drying processes, the coffee powder or granules are usually sprayed with coffee aroma concentrate. Coffee extract powder is very sensitive to damp and easily loses its aroma. Once opened it should always be kept in airtight container.

The Perfect Pot

• When making coffee always use fresh cold water and heat it to just below boiling point. If bubbling boiling water is poured over ground coffee, the coffee may easily become bitter and lose some of its aroma.

• Beans for filter coffee are usually medium ground. It is important that the coffee should not become hot while it is being ground, so traditional metal mills are not suitable.

• If you buy an espresso/cappuccino machine, you need to experiment patiently with it. The type of machine, the freshness of the beans and how finely they are ground are all crucial to achieving perfect results. The coffee blend and roast are secondary considerations. As a rule of thumb, the finer the coffee is ground the better. However, if it is too fine, the water runs through the coffee too slowly and releases bitter particles. Incidentally, the foam is not the be-all and end-all of classic cappuccino: the more freshly roasted the beans, the more delicious the coffee.

Recipe Notes

Unless stated otherwise, all recipes serve 4.

Gelatin: 4 sheets of leaf gelatin are equal to 1 tablespoon of granulated unsweetened gelatin. One envelope of granulated gelatin = $1/4$ ounce = about $2^1/2$ teaspoons. Two non-animal sources of thickening agent are Carrageen, a gelatinous substance derived from seaweed and Agar (also agar-agar, kanten and Japanese gelatin), a dried seaweed sold in blocks, powder and strands that is used as a setting agent. Agar has stronger setting properties than gelatin, so use less when substituting.

Ice cream: several recipes use an ice-cream maker. If you do not have one, beat the ice cream at least three times during freezing, at intervals of between 20 minutes and 1 hour. Pour the mixture into a plastic container and place it in the freezer for 1 hour, or until ice crystals are beginning to form around the edge. Turn the mixture into a bowl and beat well to break up the crystals, then return it to the container and freeze again. Repeat the process twice more at hourly intervals, then return the ice cream to the freezer until solid. Finally, leave it to freeze completely. About 30 minutes before serving, remove from the freezer and allow to soften in the refrigerator, then stir until smooth. If required, cut into portions at this stage and return to the refrigerator.

'Strong, rich coffee cheers

me up, gives me energy,

exceptional strength and

desire for action.'

Napoleon Bonaparte, Emperor of the French (1769-1821)

The way we drink coffee is changing. It is now being enriched with extra aromas to become a fashion item. When the coffee comes out of the coffee-maker or espresso machine, an aromatic syrup can be added. For filter coffee or coffee made by water being poured on to it, the aromatic syrup can be mixed with the ground coffee.

Cappuccino and Milky Coffee

White coffee with creamy whisked milk is delicious. The simplest way of making it is by whisking the milk with a hand-held electric whisk while it is heating up. If you have a coffee machine with a steam-device, you can also froth the milk by using steam. If you are really sold on foaming milk, you can buy a small electric foaming device.

Foamy Cinnamon Milk

Serves 1
7 tbsp full-cream milk
1 cinnamon stick
1 cup freshly brewed coffee
ground cinnamon, for sprinkling

1 *Bring the milk to the boil with the cinnamon stick in a small pan.*
2 *Remove the cinnamon stick and whisk the milk until it is foamy.*
3 *Pour the cinnamon foam onto the coffee. Sift a little ground cinnamon on top.*

Frothy Vanilla Milk

Serves 1
$1/2$ vanilla pod
7 tbsp full-cream milk
$1/8$ cup / 25 g / 1 oz vanilla sugar
1 cup freshly brewed coffee

1 *Halve the vanilla pod lengthways and scrape out the seeds.*
2 *Pour the milk into a pan, add the vanilla seeds and vanilla sugar and bring to the boil, whisking constantly.*
3 *Pour the vanilla foam onto the coffee.*

Photo right: Frothy Vanilla Milk and Fritters with Coffee Ricotta Filling (see page 121).

Hot Chocolate with Coffee and Cinnamon

Serves 4

5 oz / 150 g / 5 oz plain chocolate

1 1/2 cups / 400 ml /14 fl oz milk

3/4 oz / 20 g / 3/4 oz cocoa
  powder

7 tbsp water

1 cinnamon stick

7 tbsp freshly brewed strong
  coffee

1 Chop the chocolate into small pieces.

2 Put all the ingredients into a saucepan and bring to the boil. Lower the heat and simmer gently for about 15 minutes. Strain into a bowl, cover and leave to cool.

3 To serve, reheat the mixture, whisking constantly, but do not allow it to boil.

T i p :

Preparing the chocolate in advance and then reheating it to serve makes it creamier and more aromatic.

Photo right: Hot Chocolate with Coffee and Cinnamon.

Nutmeg Coriander Foam

Serves 1

1/2 tsp coriander seeds

7 tbsp full-cream milk

1 tsp Ginger Nutmeg Syrup
  (see page 62)

1 cup freshly brewed coffee

freshly grated nutmeg, for
sprinkling

1 Lightly crush the coriander seeds with a mortar and pestle. Place in a pan with the milk and the ginger-nutmeg syrup and bring to the boil. Strain the milk into a jug and whisk until foamy.

2 Pour the nutmeg coriander foam over the coffee. Sprinkle with a pinch of grated nutmeg.

Stay-awake Coffee

Serves 1

2 free-range egg yolks

$1/8$ cup / 25 g / 1 oz sugar

**7 tbsp freshly brewed, strong
coffee**

**1 tbsp Sweet Coffee Essence
(see page 56)**

1 *Put the egg yolks and sugar in
a heatproof bowl and beat
together until light and fluffy.*

2 *Place the bowl over a pan of
barely simmering water and
gradually add the coffee,
whisking constantly. Continue
whisking until the mixture is
thick and foamy.*

3 *Pour the coffee essence into a
glass and top up with the beaten
egg and coffee mixture. Serve
immediately.*

Coffee Granita*

Serves 4

2 cups / 500 ml / 18 fl oz freshly brewed strong coffee

¹/₂ apple, peeled, cored and chopped

8 coriander seeds, lightly crushed

1 tsp finely grated orange rind

1 tbsp Sweet Coffee Essence (see page 56)

¹/₄ cup / 40 g / 1¹/₂ oz sugar

2 tbsp Irish whiskey

candied orange peel, to decorate

1 *Put the coffee, apple, coriander seeds, orange rind and coffee essence in a pan and bring to the boil. Continue boiling until reduced to 1¹/₄ cups/300 ml/¹/₂ pint.*

2 *Remove the pan from the heat and stir in the sugar and whiskey. Pour the mixture into a shallow container, leave to cool and then place in the freezer for 30 minutes.*

3 *Remove from the freezer and beat with a fork to break up the ice crystals. Return to the freezer. Beat the mixture with a fork every 20 minutes until it has frozen into fine ice crystals.*

4 *To serve, spoon the granita into chilled glasses and decorate with candied orange peel.*

*a grainy frozen mixture of sugar, water and a flavored liquid, such as coffee or lemon juice.

Coffee Topped with Chili Foam

Serves 4

2¹/₂ cups / 600 ml / 1 pint freshly
  brewed strong coffee
4 tbsp Mexican Spicy Syrup
  (see page 60)

For the topping:
7 tbsp double cream
1 free-range egg yolk
1 tsp chili powder

1 *Preheat the oven to
220°C/425°F/Gas Mark 7.*
2 *To make the topping, whisk 3
tbsp of the cream until stiff.*
3 *Bring the remaining cream to
the boil, then whisk it into the
egg yolk in a heatproof bowl.
Add the chili powder, set the
bowl over a pan of barely
simmering water and whisk until
thickened.*
4 *Remove the bowl from the
heat and gently fold in the
whipped cream.*
5 *Divide the coffee among four
ovenproof cups or ramekins and
stir 1 tbsp syrup into each. Spoon
the topping over each cup or
ramekin and bake for a few
minutes until golden on top.*

Mexican Spicy Coffee

Serves 1

1 tablespoon Mexican Spicy
  Syrup (see page 60)
1 cup freshly brewed double-
  strength coffee
1 tbsp double cream, whipped

*Put the syrup into a coffee cup
and pour the coffee on top. Add
the whipped cream and serve
immediately.*

*Photo right: Coffee Topped with Chili
Foam.*

Exotic Mocha Bowl

Serves 8

7 tbsp Orange Vanilla Syrup
  (see page 60)
7 tbsp Hot Coffee Essence (see
  page 56)
1^1/$_4$ cups / 300 ml / ^{1}/$_2$ pint rum
10 thin strips of fresh root ginger
2^3/$_4$ cups / 700 ml / 1^1/$_4$ pints
  sparkling white wine, chilled

for the decoration:
1 cup / 150 g / 5 oz pineapple
  cubes, drained if canned
^{1}/$_2$ cup / 50 g / 2 oz
  pomegranate seeds

1 *Put the orange syrup and
coffee essence into a pan, set
over a low heat but do not allow
to boil. Add the rum and ginger.
Remove from the heat, pour into
a large bowl, cover and leave to
cool. Chill in the refrigerator for
12 hours.*
2 *Add the pineapple cubes and
pomegranate seeds to the
mixture, top with the sparkling
wine and serve chilled.*

Coffee Frappé

Serves 1

3^3/$_4$ oz / 100 g / 3^3/$_4$ oz
  Coffee Parfait (see page 102)
^{2}/$_3$ cup / 150 ml / ^{1}/$_4$ pint
  cold strong coffee
1 tablespoon coffee liqueur
2 tbsp double cream, lightly
  whipped
chocolate chips, to decorate
  (optional)

1 *Put the parfait into a mixing
bowl, add the coffee and liqueur
and beat with an electric mixer
for 2 minutes. Add the whipped
cream and briefly beat again.*
2 *Spoon the frappé into a tall glass.
Decorate with chocolate chips.*

'Hot as hell,

black as the devil,

pure as an angel

and sweet as love –

that's how coffee must be.'

Charles, Duke of Talleyrand, French politician (1754-1838)

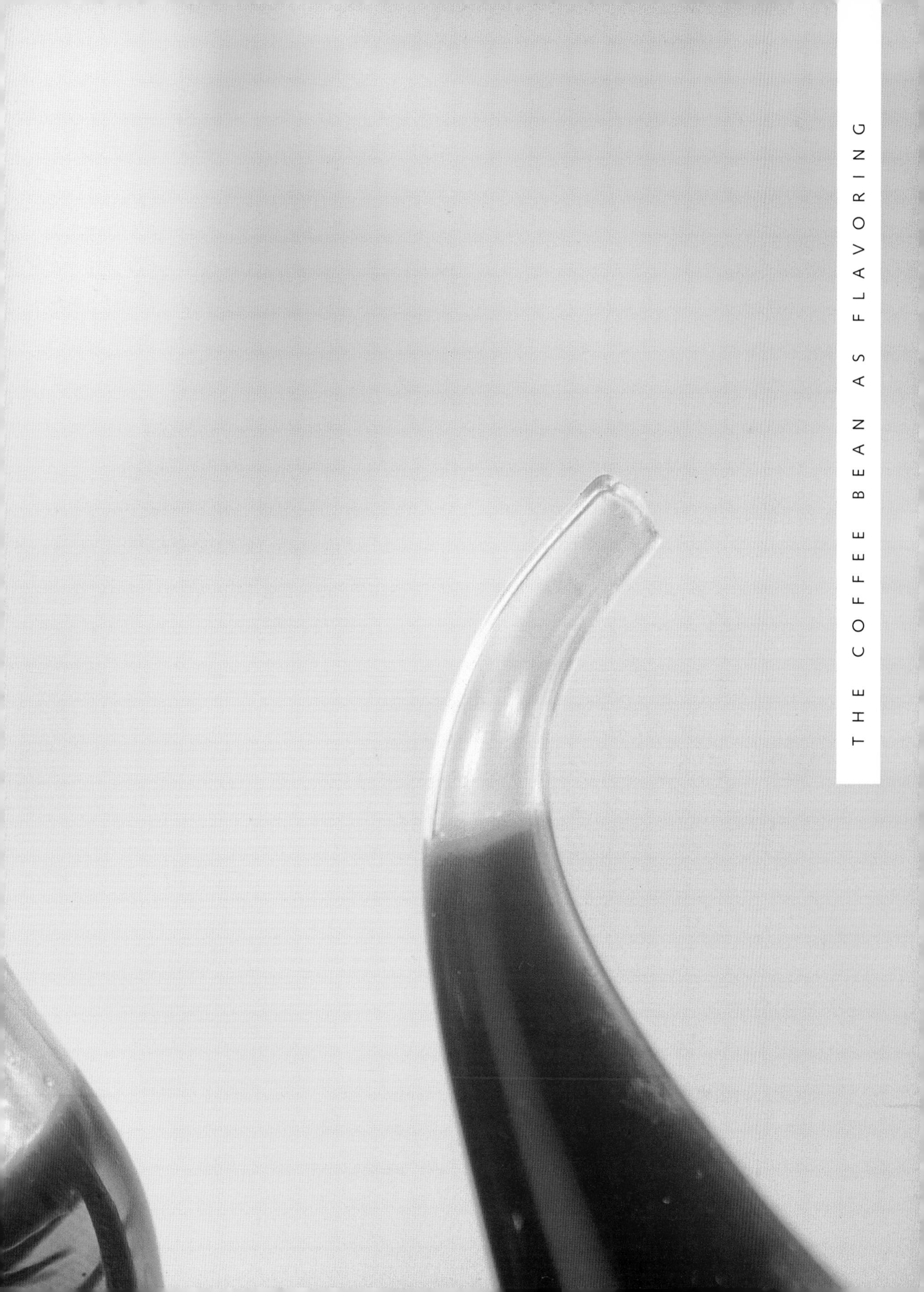

The coffee bean is an enhancer and a mysterious aromatic flavoring in both savory and sweet dishes. The coffee essences should be used sparingly, as the caffeine content is not lowered in the thick reduced mixture.

Sweet Coffee Essence

3 tbsp castor sugar
$^3/_4$ cup / 200 ml / 7 fl oz freshly brewed strong coffee

Heat the sugar in a heavy-based pan until it melts and turns golden brown. Stir in the coffee and cook over a high heat until reduced to $^1/_4$ cup/50 ml/2 fl oz.
U s e
To flavor soft ice cream, including parfaits, mousses and cakes.

Fruity Coffee Essence

2 cups / 500 ml / 18 fl oz apple juice
10 coffee beans, ground
5 coriander seeds, crushed
$^1/_2$ cinnamon stick
pinch of cayenne pepper

Put all the ingredients into a pan, bring to the boil and cook until syrupy. Strain through a fine sieve.
U s e
For an unusual flavoring in salad dressings or add sparingly to fried prawns.

Hot Coffee Essence

$^3/_4$ cup / 200 ml / 7 fl oz freshly brewed strong coffee
2 tbsp maple syrup
$^1/_4$ cup / 20 g / $^3/_4$ oz finely chopped fresh root ginger
$^1/_2$ fresh chili, seeded and finely chopped
2 tbsp balsamic vinegar

Put all the ingredients into a pan, bring to the boil and cook until syrupy. Strain through a fine sieve.
U s e
Add sparingly to fruit desserts. For example, add 2-3 drops to fresh strawberries or drizzle over fresh pineapple.

Mexican Spice Paste

1/2 egg-plant/aubergine, peeled
   and diced
1 tbsp extra virgin olive oil
1 fresh poblano chili, seeded
   and diced
4 fresh serrano chilies, seeded
   and diced
2 hot red chilies, seeded and
   diced
1 tbsp sea salt
2 tbsp diced fresh root ginger
1 garlic clove, crushed
2 tbsp Balsamic Mocha
   (see page 63)
1 tbsp Hot Coffee Essence
   (see page 56)

*1 Blanch the egg-plant/aubergine
cubes in lightly salted boiling
water for 1-2 minutes. Drain and
press out any excess water.*
*2 Heat the oil in a pan. Add the
egg-plant/aubergine and all the
chilies and cook over a medium
heat, stirring occasionally, until
lightly browned. Sprinkle with
the salt, lower the heat, cover
and simmer gently for 10
minutes, until softened.*
*3 Add all the remaining
ingredients and cook, stirring
constantly, until the mixture
binds into a paste.*

*4 Spoon the paste into a
sterilized screw-top jar and leave
to cool. Store it in the
refrigerator.*
U s e
*Use as a condiment or to spice
up soups.*

Spicy Praline

Butter or margarine, for greasing
1/4 cup / 40 g / 1 1/2 oz castor
   sugar
1 tsp coffee beans, ground
2 tsp / 10 g / 1/4 oz pistachio nuts
1 tsp coriander seeds, crushed
1 tsp finely grated orange rind

*1 Grease a baking sheet with
butter/margarine.*
*2 Heat the sugar in a heavy-
based pan until it melts and
turns golden brown. Add all the
remaining ingredients and stir
well. Tip the mixture onto the
baking sheet and spread to about
1/4 in/5 mm thick, then leave to
cool and set.*
*3 Finely chop the praline before
using.*
U s e
*For creamy desserts and soft ice
creams, including parfaits, and as
a decoration for cakes.*

Coffee Praline

Butter or margarine, for greasing
1/4 cup / 40 g / 1 1/2 oz castor
   sugar
1/4 cup / 50 g / 2 oz dark-roasted
   coffee beans, coarsely chopped

*1 Grease a baking sheet with
butter/margarine.*
*2 Heat the sugar in a heavy-
based pan until it melts and turns
golden brown.*
*3 Add the coffee beans and stir.
Turn out the mixture onto the
baking sheet, spread out and
leave to cool.*
*4 Finely chop the praline before
using.*
U s e
*For creamy desserts and soft ice
creams, including parfaits, and to
sprinkle on frappés*

*Photos right, clockwise from top:
Spicy Praline, Coffee Praline, Coffee
Marinade (see page 60) and Mexican
Spice Paste*

Syrup

For many years, espresso and other types of coffee have been enlivened by the addition of other aromatic flavors. The two syrups here each add a new lift to everyday coffee.

Coffee Marinade

7 tbsp Coffee Vanilla Oil
 (see page 63)
1 tsp Hot Coffee Essence
 (see page 56)
1 tbsp pink peppercorns
1 tbsp black peppercorns
pinch of ground cumin
2 sun-dried tomatoes in oil,
 drained and thinly sliced
1 garlic clove, thinly sliced

1 *Mix all the ingredients together in a bowl and leave to stand for 1 hour.*
U s e
As a marinade for poultry and rabbit.

Orange Vanilla Syrup

³/₄ cup / 200 ml / 7 fl oz freshly
 squeezed orange juice
1¹/₄ cups / 300 ml / ¹/₂ pint water
1¹/₄ cups / 250 g / 9 oz castor sugar
2 vanilla pods
10 lime flowers (from health
 store or herbalist)

1 *Put the orange juice, water and sugar into a pan. Slit the vanilla pods lengthways, scrape out the seeds and add them to the pan together with the lime flowers. Add one of the vanilla pods to the pan and place the other in a sterilized bottle.*
2 *Bring the liquid to the boil over a medium heat and boil until reduced to about 1 cup/250 ml/8 fl oz. Strain into a jug, then pour it into the prepared bottle while still hot.*
U s e
To add a sophisticated touch to espressos or mocha frappés.

Mexican Spicy Syrup

2 cups / 500 ml / 18 fl oz water
¹/₂ cup / 100 g / 3³/₄ oz
 piloncillo (Mexican brown sugar)
 or soft dark brown sugar
1 cup / 200 g / 7 oz castor sugar
1 fresh chili, slit lengthways and
 seeded
2 tbsp coriander seeds
2 tbsp crushed black peppercorns
1 cinnamon stick

1 *Put the water and both types of sugar into a pan and bring to the boil, stirring until the sugar has dissolved. Continue to boil over a low heat until the liquid has reduced by half. Add the remaining ingredients to the sugar syrup, return to the boil, then pour into a sterilized bottle.*
2 *Store the syrup in a dark place for 2 weeks before using.*
U s e
For Mexican Spicy Coffee (see page 50) to give a boost. Add sparingly to sauces and salsas.

Photo right:
Mexican Spicy Syrup
Photo far right: Orange Vanilla Syrup

Ginger Nutmeg Syrup

2 cups / 500 ml / 18 fl oz water

1¹/₄ cups / 250 g / 9 oz castor
  sugar

¹/₄ cup / 50 g / 2 oz fresh root
  ginger, peeled

6 kumquats

1 tsp ground mace

¹/₂ tsp freshly grated nutmeg

¹/₂ tsp ground nutmeg

1 *Put the water and sugar into a
pan. Finely grate in about ¹/₂
oz/15 g of the ginger. Bring the
liquid to the boil, stirring until
the sugar has dissolved. Continue
to boil until the liquid has
reduced by half.*

2 *Thinly slice the remaining ginger.
Thinly slice the kumquats, without
peeling, and remove the pips.*

3 *Add the sliced ginger,
kumquats and spices to the syrup
and bring back to the boil. Pour
the syrup into a sterilized jar and
seal. Leave to mature for 2 weeks
in a warm dark place before using.*

U s e

To spice up coffee or cappuccino.

Balsamic Mocha

$^1/_4$ cup / 40 g / $1^1/_2$ oz castor
  sugar
2 tbsp / 20 g / $^3/_4$ oz piloncillo
  (Mexican brown sugar) or soft
  dark brown sugar
2 tsp Fruity Coffee Essence
  (see page 56)
7 tbsp balsamic vinegar
2 cups / 500 ml / 18 fl oz cider
  vinegar
1 tbsp coffee beans
3 thin slices of ginger
1 cinnamon stick

1 *Heat the castor sugar in a
heavy-based pan until it melts
and turns golden brown. Add the
brown sugar and coffee essence,
then stir in the balsamic vinegar
and bring to the boil. Lower the
heat and boil until the liquid is
reduced to $^1/_4$ cup/50 ml/2 fl oz.
Add the cider vinegar and pour the
mixture into a sterilized bottle.
Add the coffee beans, ginger and
cinnamon stick and seal.*
2 *Leave the bottle to stand for a
week on a sunny windowsill.*
Use
*To spice up sauces, salad dressings
and to add sparingly to coffee.*

Coffee Vanilla Oil

1 vanilla pod
1 tbsp coffee beans (espresso
  roast), ground
1 tbsp pink peppercorns
3 drops coffee essence
$1^1/_4$ cups / 300 ml / $^1/_2$ pint
  grapeseed oil

1 *Slit the vanilla pod lengthways
and scrape out the seeds. Put the
pod, seeds and all the other
ingredients into a sterilized
bottle. Seal and shake gently.*
2 *Leave to stand at room
temperature in a dark place for 4
days, then store in the refrigerator.*
Use
*To put the finishing touch to
salad dressing, Mexican sauces
and spicy peperonatas, the
delicious Italian mix of peppers,
tomatoes, onions and garlic.*

Photo left: Balsamic Mocha
Photo far left: Coffee Vanilla Oil

'He was my cream, and I was his coffee,

And when you poured us together,

it was something.'

Josephine Baker, US singer and civil rights activist (1906-1975)

Asparagus in Puff Pastry Rings with Coffee Orange Butter

STARTER

4 oz / 115 g / 4 oz puff pastry,
thawed if frozen
1 egg yolk, lightly beaten
16 green asparagus spears
8-12 white asparagus spears*
1 tsp castor sugar
1 tbsp / 15 g / ^{1}/$_2$ oz butter
or margarine
sea salt

Coffee orange butter:
1 vanilla pod
7 tbsp freshly squeezed
orange juice
10 coffee beans, ground
2 tbsp / 25 g / 1 oz cold
butter, diced
cayenne pepper
fresh chervil sprigs, to garnish

*use green asparagus if you
cannot obtain this.

Preheat the oven to 200°C/400°F/Gas Mark 6.

1 Roll out the puff pastry to ^{1}/$_2$ in/1 cm thick and stamp out 4 rounds with a 2-in/5-cm cutter. Stamp out the centers with a smaller cutter to make rings. Place the pastry rings on a baking sheet and brush with egg yolk. Bake for 10 minutes.

2 Peel the lower parts of the green asparagus spears. Trim off the coarse lower stems of the green and white asparagus, making the spears the same length. Use the trimmings in a risotto, vegetable stew or soup.

3 Pour 2 cups/500 ml/18 fl oz water into a pan, add the sugar and butter with a pinch of sea salt and bring to the boil. Lower the heat, add the white asparagus, cover and cook for 15 minutes. Remove the asparagus with a slotted spoon and drain on kitchen paper. Reserve ^{1}/$_4$ cup/ 50 ml/2 fl oz of the cooking liquid.

4 Meanwhile, add the green asparagus to a large pan of lightly salted boiling water, cover and cook for 5 minutes over a low heat. Remove the asparagus with a slotted spoon and drain on kitchen paper.

5 For the mocha orange butter, slit the vanilla pod lengthways and scrape out the seeds. Put the vanilla pod, seeds, orange juice and coffee in a pan. Add the reserved asparagus cooking liquid and bring to the boil. Lower the heat and cook until reduced to ^{1}/$_4$ cup/50 ml/2 fl oz. Strain into a clean pan. Just before serving, gently reheat the sauce beating in the diced butter a little at a time. Do not allow the sauce to boil.

6 Arrange the white and green asparagus in the puff pastry rings. Pour over the coffee orange butter and garnish with chervil.

Stuffed Onions with Coffee Balsamic Butter

STARTER

4 large onions

Stuffing:
1 green pepper, seeded and diced
1 red pepper, seeded and diced
1 yellow pepper, seeded and diced
1 small kohlrabi, finely diced
2 tbsp cooked wild rice
2 tbsp cooked buckwheat
2 tbsp double cream
1 tbsp grated Parmesan cheese
7 tbsp hot vegetable stock
herbed sea salt
freshly ground black pepper

Coffee balsamic butter:
7 tbsp balsamic vinegar
7 tbsp apple juice
10 coriander seeds, crushed
$1/2$ fresh chili, seeded and finely chopped
10 coffee beans, ground
2 tbsp / 20 g / 3 oz butter or margarine, chilled

Preheat the oven to 180°C/350°F/Gas Mark 4.

1 Blanch the onions in lightly salted boiling water for 5 minutes. Remove with a slotted spoon and reserve the cooking liquid. Cut a 'lid' off each onion, then scoop out the flesh from the center, leaving just three layers. Take care not to pierce the onion shells. Finely chop the scooped-out flesh.

2 Bring the reserved onion cooking liquid back to the boil and blanch the peppers and kohlrabi for 2 minutes. Drain well and place in a bowl. Add the chopped onion, rice, buckwheat, cream and Parmesan, season with herbed salt and pepper and mix well. Divide the mixture among the onion shells and replace the 'lids'.

3 Place the stuffed onions in an ovenproof dish, pour in the hot vegetable stock and braise for 30 minutes. Transfer the stuffed onions to a plate, cover and keep warm.

4 For the coffee balsamic butter, pour the vinegar and apple juice into a small pan, add the coriander seeds, chili and coffee and bring to the boil over a high heat. Continue to boil until the liquid has reduced by half. Stir in the vegetable stock from the onion dish. Strain through a fine sieve into a clean pan. Bring to the boil over a high heat and continue to boil until the liquid has reduced to $1/4$ cup/50 ml/2 fl oz. Just before serving stir in the cold butter but do not allow the sauce to boil. Season with herbed salt.

5 To serve, spoon a little of the sauce onto each of four serving plates in a decorative pattern and top with the stuffed onions.

Coffee Rice Balls with Shiitake Mushrooms and Pepper Coulis/sauce

STARTER

Coffee rice balls:

1 tbsp extra virgin olive oil

$^3/_8$ cup / 75 g / 3 oz risotto rice

7 tbsp vegetable stock

$^2/_3$ cup / 150 ml / $^1/_4$ pint freshly brewed strong coffee

1 tbsp finely chopped fresh root ginger

1 small onion, finely chopped

1 small bunch of parsley, finely chopped

vegetable oil, for frying

Pepper coulis/sauce:

7 tbsp vegetable stock

1 red or yellow or green pepper, seeded and chopped

$1^1/_2$ tsp millet flakes

1 fresh oregano sprig

pinch of ground cumin

1 tsp acacia honey

1 tsp white wine vinegar

sea salt

freshly ground white pepper

Shiitake mushrooms:

1 tsp butter

2 tbsp dry white wine

1 tbsp soy sauce

8 small shiitake mushrooms

1 *Heat the olive oil in a heavy-based pan. Add the rice and cook, stirring constantly, over a medium heat, until all the grains are coated and glistening. Pour in the vegetable stock and coffee, add the ginger and onion and bring to the boil. Cover, turn off the heat but leave the pan to stand on the stove for about 30 minutes, until the rice is tender.*

2 *Stir in the parsley. Knead the mixture vigorously. Form 16 equal-sized balls between the palms of your hands. When you are ready to serve, heat the vegetable oil in a frying pan, add the rice balls and cook, turning frequently, until golden brown all over.*

3 *Meanwhile, make the pepper coulis. Pour the vegetable stock into a pan, add the pepper, millet flakes and oregano and bring to the boil. Lower the heat and simmer for 10 minutes. Remove and discard the oregano. Process the mixture in a blender or food processor to a fine purée and return to a clean pan.*

4 *When you are ready to serve, bring the coulis back to the boil, stir in the cumin, honey and vinegar and season with sea salt and pepper.*

5 *Meanwhile, cut off and discard the mushroom stalks. Melt the butter with the white wine and soy sauce in a small pan. Add the mushroom caps, cover and cook over a low heat for about 5 minutes, until tender. Season with pepper.*

6 *Arrange the fried rice balls with the braised mushrooms and pepper coulis on serving plates.*

Ricotta Coffee Ravioli with Strawberry Coulis/sauce

STARTER

Serves 4
Dough:
$^3/_4$ cup / 90 g / $3^1/_2$ oz plain flour, plus extra for dusting
$^1/_3$ cup / 40 g / $1^1/_2$ oz strong white bread flour
1 free-range egg
1 tbsp extra virgin olive oil
1 tbsp water
1 tsp instant coffee powder
$^1/_2$ teaspoon sea salt

Filling:
3 tbsp ricotta cheese
$^1/_2$ cup / 75 g / 3 oz pecorino cheese, grated
2 tbsp grated Parmesan cheese
1 tbsp finely chopped leek, green part only
2 tablespoons pine nuts, roasted and chopped
freshly grated nutmeg
chili powder

Strawberry coulis/sauce:
$1^1/_2$ cups / 250 g / 9 oz strawberries
1 tsp sugar
$^1/_2$ fresh red chili, seeded and finely chopped
4 fresh mint leaves, finely chopped
1 tsp cold butter or margarine
freshly ground black pepper

1 *For the ravioli dough, sift both types of flour onto a work surface and make a well in the center. Whisk together the egg, olive oil, water, instant coffee and salt and pour them into the well. Gradually incorporate the flour into the liquid and knead to a firm dough. Wrap in Saran wrap/clingfilm and leave to rest in the refrigerator for 1 hour.*
2 *For the stuffing, mix together all the cheeses, the leek and pine nuts and season to taste with nutmeg and chili powder. Leave to stand for 30 minutes.*
3 *Divide the ravioli dough in half. Roll out one portion on a lightly floured surface to about $^1/_{16}$ in/1 mm thick and cut into strips about $1^1/_2$ in/4 cm wide. Sprinkle them with water. Place walnut-size portions of the stuffing at $1^1/_2$ in/4 cm intervals on the dough strips. Roll out the second portion of dough and cut into strips. Place the uncovered dough strips over the filling and press down firmly between the mounds and around the edges. Cut out triangles using a pastry wheel. Lightly dust a baking sheet with flour and place the ravioli on it, then dust lightly with flour.*

4 *For the strawberry coulis, place the strawberries and sugar in a pan and cook over a low heat for 10 minutes. Push through a fine sieve into a clean pan. Reduce the strawberry juice to about 7 tbsp over a low heat. Add the chili, season with pepper and cook for a further 3 minutes over a low heat. Just before serving stir in the mint leaves and the butter, but do not allow the coulis to boil.*
5 *Meanwhile, bring a large pan of lightly salted water to the boil. Add the ravioli, bring back to the boil and cook until they rise to the surface. Leave to stand for 1-2 minutes. Remove them from the pan with a slotted spoon and arrange on serving plates with the strawberry coulis.*

Serving suggestion
Serve with young asparagus tips, also known as sprue, and green peas.

Coffee Roulade with Salmon Filling and Apple and Horseradish Confit

Roulade:

2 free-range eggs, separated
1 tablespoon Hot Coffee Essence
(see page 56)
large pinch of ground coriander
large pinch of grated fresh
root ginger
pinch of sea salt
$^1/_2$ cup / 50 g / 2 oz plain flour
large pinch of baking powder
2 tbsp / 20 g / $^3/_4$ oz butter or
margarine, melted

Filling:

1 cup / 200 g / 7 oz gravadlax
or smoked salmon fillet
6 slices smoked salmon
1 fresh red chili, seeded and
finely chopped
2 tbsp sour cream or
crème fraîche
2 tbsp lemon juice
7 tbsp double cream
herbed sea salt
freshly ground black pepper
fresh dill, to garnish

Preheat the oven to 220°C/425°F/Gas Mark 7.

1 Line a Swiss Roll cake tin with non-stick wax/greaseproof paper.

2 Beat together the egg yolks, coffee essence, 1 tsp herbed salt, the coriander and ginger until pale and fluffy. Beat the egg whites with the pinch of salt in a clean grease-free bowl until stiff. Sift the flour with the baking powder into another bowl. Gradually fold the flour into the egg yolk mixture, alternating with the egg whites. Spoon the mixture into the prepared tin and spread out to about $^1/_4$ in/5 mm thick. Bake for 5 minutes. Lift the sponge off the tin, using the wax/greaseproof paper to help; remove the paper and cover the sponge with the inverted tin. This helps it to remain moist and so easier to roll.

3 Cut a $^1/_2$-in/1-cm thick strip from the salmon fillet and set aside. Cut the remainder in half. For the salmon tartare, cut one half into small cubes and mix with the sour cream or crème fraîche, chili and 1 tbsp of the lemon juice. Season with black pepper and a little herbed salt.

Arrange the six smoked salmon slices in a rectangle on a sheet of Saran wrap/clingfilm. Spread the salmon tartare on the rectangle. Lay the salmon strip on top and roll up the salmon rectangle to enclose the filling.

4 Finely chop the remaining salmon, mix with half the cream and the remaining lemon juice and season with herbed salt and pepper. Place the mixture in a blender or food processor and process to a purée. Scoop the purée into a bowl. Whisk the remaining cream stiff and fold it into the purée to make a mousse.

5 Spread the salmon mousse on the sponge base and lay the rolled salmon on top. Fold it up, Swiss Roll fashion. Cover the roulade in Saran wrap/clingfilm and leave in a cool place for about 2 hours.

6 Slice the roulade, place on serving plates, garnish with dill and serve with the apple and horseradish confit (see opposite).

Apple and Horseradish Confit

1 eating apple

1 tbsp lemon juice

1¹/₄ cups / 300 ml / ¹/₂ pint apple juice

8 black peppercorns, crushed

10 coriander seeds, crushed

large pinch of cayenne pepper

¹/₂-in/1-cm piece of fresh horseradish, peeled and diced

1 *Halve and core the apple but do not peel. Grate one half. Chop the other half and sprinkle them both with the lemon juice. Cover and set aside.*

2 *Pour the apple juice into a pan, add the grated apple, peppercorns and coriander seeds and bring to the boil. Lower the* heat and cook until reduced to ¹/₄ cup/50 ml/2 fl oz. Push the mixture through a fine sieve into a clean pan.

3 *Add the horseradish and bring to the boil. Season with cayenne pepper and stir in the chopped apple.*

Coffee-smoked Fish with Nut Vinaigrette

STARTER

²/₃ cup / 115 g / 4 oz monkfish fillet
²/₃ cup / 115 g / 4 oz red mullet fillet
4 tbsp coffee beans, ground
1 bunch of fresh thyme, chopped
2-3 fresh rosemary sprigs, chopped
2 tomatoes, peeled and quartered
1 head frisée (curly endive or chicory) or spinach, finely chopped
2 tbsp extra virgin olive oil
4 unpeeled large new potatoes, sliced
sea salt
freshly ground black pepper

Nut vinaigrette:
1 celery stick, finely chopped
¹/₂ cup / 50 g / 2 oz hazelnuts, toasted and coarsely chopped
1 tbsp Coffee Vanilla Oil (see page 63)
1 tbsp raspberry vinegar
herbed sea salt

Preheat the oven to 220°C/425°F/Gas Mark 7.

1 Season the fish fillets with salt and pepper and place them on a rack.

2 Put the coffee and herbs into a frying pan and lay the rack of fish on top. Cover with a lid and place over a high heat. When the pan begins to smoke, turn off the heat, but leave the pan, still covered, on the stove for 20 minutes.

3 Scoop out the pulp and seeds from the tomato quarters and cut the flesh into thin strips. Place the pulp and seeds in a pan, bring to the boil, then push through a sieve into a bowl.

4 Brush a baking sheet with the oil and sprinkle with sea salt. Arrange the potato slices in a single layer on it. Roast for 15-20 minutes, until golden brown.

5 For the vinaigrette, blanch the celery in lightly salted boiling water for 1 minute, then drain and mix with all the remaining ingredients.

6 Blanch the frisée or spinach in lightly salted boiling water for 2 minutes, then drain and place in a bowl. Stir in the sieved tomato and the tomato strips and season with salt and pepper.

7 Arrange the roast potato slices on a serving plate. Pile the greens in the middle and top with the fish. Sprinkle on the nut vinaigrette and serve.

Smoked Trout Fillet with Pink Pepper Mousse

3 smoked trout fillets, about
3^1/$_2$ oz/90 g each, skinned
^{1}/$_2$ tart apple
1 bunch of fresh chives
2 tbsp low-fat curd cheese
1 tsp Mexican Spice Paste (see
page 58)
1 tsp Hot Coffee Essence (see
page 56)
1 tbsp pink peppercorns
1 tsp lemon juice
1 small baguette

Vinaigrette dressing:
1 small red onion
1 tbsp Balsamic Mocha (see
page 63) or balsamic vinegar
1 tbsp extra virgin olive oil
1 bunch of radishes
8 black olives, stoned and
chopped
1 carton cress

1 *Cut two of the trout fillets into 8 equal pieces.*
2 *Dice the third fillet and the half apple into small cubes. Cut off the best chive tips 2^1/$_2$-3 in/6-8 cm long and reserve. Finely chop the remainder.*
3 *Mix together the curd cheese, chopped chives, spice paste, coffee essence, peppercorns and lemon juice. Stir in the diced trout and apple cubes.*
4 *For the vinaigrette, chop half the onion and cut the other half into thin strips. Dice two radishes and thinly slice the remainder.*
5 *Whisk together the balsamic mocha or vinegar and olive oil,* then add the chopped onion, diced radish cubes and olives.
6 *Cut the baguette into 8 slices ^{1}/$_4$ in/5 mm thick. Toast until lightly golden on both sides.*
7 *Spread the trout mixture on to the toast. Lay the trout fillet pieces on top. Garnish with onion strips, radish slices, cress and the reserved chives. Pile one piece of topped toast on top of another to form double-deckers and serve with the vinaigrette.*

Crayfish Cappuccino Soup

STARTER

8 cooked crayfish or 1 cooked
lobster
1 tsp clarified butter
2 shallots, coarsely chopped
2 tsp tomato purée
2 tbsp millet flakes
2 tomatoes, peeled and finely
chopped
20 coffee beans, ground
1 tbsp Mexican Spice Paste (see
page 58)
2 cups / 500 ml / 18 fl oz
chicken or fish stock
1 cup / 200 ml / 7 fl oz double
cream
dash of coffee liqueur
cayenne pepper

1 *Cut off, peel and reserve the crayfish tails. Discard the heads, peel the bodies and coarsely chop the flesh. If using a lobster, prepare in the same way.*
2 *Melt the butter in a heavy-based pan, add the shallots and cook over a low heat, stirring occasionally, until softened and glazed. Add the tomato purée and millet flakes and cook, stirring constantly, until golden brown. Add the chopped crayfish, tomatoes, coffee and spice paste. Pour in the stock, bring to the boil and simmer over a medium heat for 20 minutes. Push the mixture through a fine sieve with the back of a wooden spoon into a clean pan.*
3 *Whisk $^1/_4$ cup/50 ml/2 fl oz of the cream until stiff.*

4 *Lightly steam the crayfish tails until warmed through and place them in individual soup bowls.*
5 *Add the remaining cream to the soup and bring to the boil. Stir in the liqueur and season with cayenne pepper. Stir in the whipped cream and whisk the soup until foamy. Ladle into the bowls and serve.*

Chestnut Coffee Soup
with a Pastry Lid

STARTER

1 tbsp extra virgin olive oil
$^1/_2$ cup / 50 g / 2 oz smoked
bacon, diced
1 shallot, finely chopped
1 cup / 100 g / 3$^3/_4$ oz peeled
chestnuts, drained if canned and
thawed if frozen
1$^1/_4$ cups / 300 ml / $^1/_2$ pint
vegetable stock
1$^1/_4$ cups / 300 ml / $^1/_2$ pint
freshly brewed strong coffee
1 tbsp diced celery
1 tbsp diced carrot
1 tbsp thin strips of leek
7 tbsp double cream, stiffly
whipped
Balsamic Mocha to taste (see
page 63)
12-16 oz / 350-450 g / 12-16 oz
puff pastry dough, thawed if
frozen
2 egg yolks, lightly beaten
sea salt
freshly ground black pepper

1 *Heat the olive oil gently in a heavy-based pan. Add the bacon and cook, stirring frequently, until crisp. Add the shallot and chestnuts and cook for a further 3 minutes. Pour in the stock and coffee and bring to the boil. Lower the heat and simmer for 20-30 minutes, until the chestnuts are tender but not mushy. Using a slotted spoon, remove and reserve a few chestnuts. Pour the soup into a blender or food processor and process to a purée. Transfer to a bowl and stir in the celery, carrot, leek and cream. Season with salt and pepper and add balsamic mocha to taste. Put the whole chestnuts into individual ovenproof soup bowls, ladle in the soup and leave to cool.*
2 *Preheat the oven to 180°C/350°F/Gas Mark 4.*
3 *Roll out the dough and cut out rounds about $^3/_4$ in/2 cm larger in diameter than the rims of the soup bowls. Brush the pastry rounds all over with egg yolk. Place the rounds, yolk side downwards, on top of the soup bowls and press them on. Cut four dough strips about $^1/_4$ in/5 mm wide, brush with yolk and press them around the soup bowls. Brush the pastry lids also.*
4 *Put the soup bowls on a baking sheet and bake for about 15 minutes, until the pastry is puffed up and golden brown.*

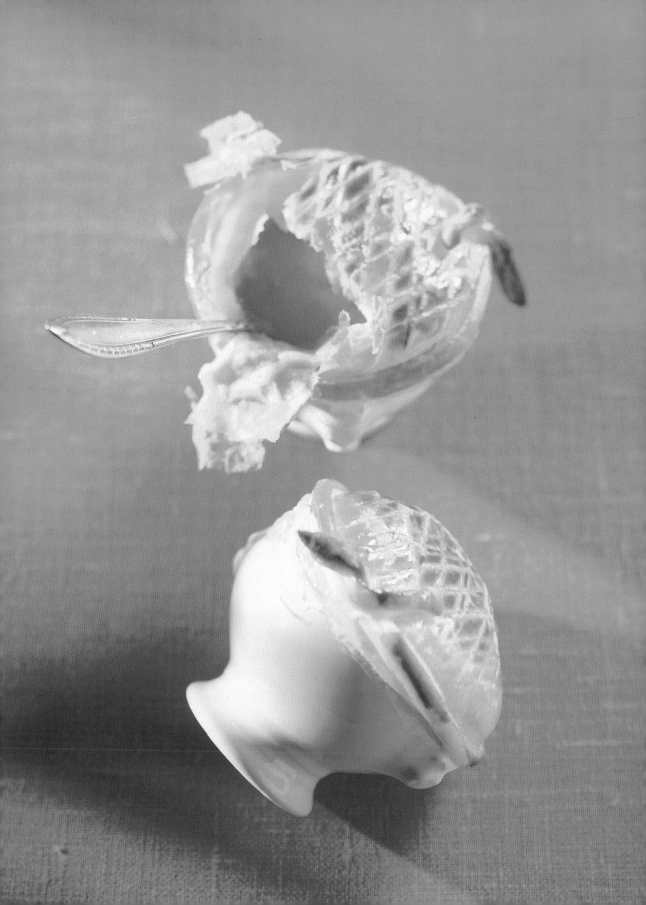

Braised Beef with Falafel and Mango Chutney

MAIN DISH

1 tsp freshly ground black pepper

grated rind of ¹/₂ orange

1 tablespoon dried thyme

4 chuck or blade beef steaks, 5 oz/150 g each

2 scallions/spring onions

2 tbsp extra virgin olive oil

1 onion, finely chopped

¹/₄ cup / 50 ml / 2 fl oz vegetable stock

2 tbsp Balsamic Mocha (see page 63)

7 tbsp red wine

7 tbsp beef consommé

1 quantity Mexican Spice Paste (see page 58)

1 *Mix together the black pepper, orange rind and dried thyme in a small bowl and rub it all over the steaks.*

2 *Trim the scallions/spring onions to the same length, cut them in half lengthways and remove the tough outer layers. Heat 1 tbsp of the olive oil in a non-stick frying pan over a medium heat. Add the scallions/spring onions and cook until softened. Add the chopped onion and cook for about 5 minutes. Add the steaks and vegetable stock, cover and cook for 5 minutes. Remove the scallions/spring onions and set aside. Pour the balsamic mocha,* wine and consommé over the steaks. Cover and braise over a medium heat for 30 minutes, or until the steak is tender. Transfer the steak to a plate and keep warm.

3 *Simmer the sauce over a low heat until reduced to about ¹/₂ cup/120 ml/4 fl oz. Stir in the spice paste and bring to the boil. Return steaks to the pan and spoon the sauce over them. Lay the scallions/spring onions on top, cover and warm through. Arrange the steaks on serving plates together with the scallions/spring onions, falafel (see opposite) and mango chutney (see below).*

Mango Chutney

1 tablespoon soft dark brown sugar

juice of ¹/₂ orange

2 tbsp / 20 g / ³/₄ oz diced fresh green chili

1 shallot, finely chopped

1 tsp diced fresh root ginger

1 cup / 130 g / 4¹/₂ oz finely diced mango

1 tbsp Hot Coffee Essence (see page 56)

Heat the sugar in a heavy-based pan until it melts. Pour in the orange juice, cover and bring to the boil. Add the chili, shallot and ginger and simmer over a low heat for 5 minutes. Add the mango and heat through. Stir in the coffee essence, cover, remove from the heat and leave to cool.

SIDE DISH

Falafel

2¹/₃ cups / 115 g / 4 oz dried garbanzos/chickpeas, soaked overnight in cold water
1 tbsp extra virgin olive oil
¹/₂ cup / 50 g / 2 oz onions, finely chopped
1 garlic clove, crushed
1 tsp chopped fresh cilantro/coriander
1 tsp ground cumin
1¹/₂ tsp tahini sesame seed paste
soy or sunflower oil, for frying

1 *Drain the garbanzos/chickpeas, then remove the tough outer skins by rubbing them hard in a dish towel.*
2 *Heat the olive oil in a frying pan. Add the onions and garlic and cook over a low heat, stirring occasionally, for about 5 minutes, until softened. Spoon the onion mixture into a blender* or food processor, add the garbanzos/chickpeas, cilantro/coriander, cumin and tahini and process to a purée.
3 *Scrape out the mixture and form into 12 balls. Heat the soy or sunflower oil in a heavy-based pan. Add the falafel and cook, turning frequently, until golden brown all over.*

Tofu Coffee Loaf with Clear Chili Sauce

MAIN DISH
(for a cake tin 9 in/22 cm long)

butter or margarine, for greasing
sesame seeds, for sprinkling
²/₃ cup / 100 g / 3³/₄ oz couscous
7 tbsp freshly brewed strong coffee,
cooled
¹/₄ cup / 40 ml / 2 fl oz water
1 tbsp extra virgin olive oil
1 tsp sea salt
1 cup / 50 g / 2 oz mushrooms,
thinly sliced
³/₄ cup / 50 g / 2 oz red peppers,
seeded and finely chopped
1 small carrot, finely grated
1 tsp Madras curry powder
1¹/₄ cups / 200 g / 7 oz firm tofu,
drained and finely mashed
¹/₄ cup / 25 g / 1 oz cashew nuts,
chopped
1 bunch of fresh chives, finely chopped
1 free-range egg
2 tbsp low-fat curd cheese

Chili sauce:
1 red pepper, seeded and finely
chopped
1 small onion, finely chopped
1 garlic clove, crushed
1 fresh chili, seeded and chopped
1¹/₄ cups / 300 ml / ¹/₂ pint
vegetable stock
dash of fruit vinegar
1 tsp pear juice
¹/₂ tsp cornstarch/cornflour
1 tablespoon dry vermouth
2 tbsp / 20 g / ³/₄ oz butter or
margarine
herbed sea salt
freshly ground black pepper

Preheat the oven to 200°C/400°F/Gas Mark 6.

1 *Grease a 9-in/22-cm long loaf tin with butter and sprinkle with the sesame seeds.*

2 *Spread out the couscous on a work surface. Sprinkle a little cold coffee over it and work into the couscous with your fingertips. Repeat this process until all the coffee is used up. Then work in the water in the same way until the mixture is saturated. This takes about 8 minutes. Drizzle with the oil, sprinkle with the salt and work these into the mixture. Wrap the couscous in a muslin square, place in a steamer, cover and cook over a pan of boiling water for 20 minutes. Transfer the couscous to a bowl and mix in the remaining ingredients. Spoon the mixture into the prepared tin.*

3 *Bake the couscous loaf for 30 minutes, covering the top with tin foil halfway through the cooking time.*

4 *For the sauce, put the red pepper, onion, garlic and chili in a pan, add the vegetable stock and simmer over a low heat for 20 minutes. Push the mixture through a fine sieve into a clean pan. Stir in the vinegar and pear juice and heat gently. Mix the cornstarch and vermouth to a smooth paste in a small bowl, then stir into the sauce. Bring the sauce to the boil, stirring constantly, then lower the heat and stir in the butter. Season with salt and pepper and serve with the loaf.*

Tip:
Bake the loaf in a loose-based tin.

Serving suggestion
Serve with pieces of roast artichoke heart, broad beans and chili sauce.

Chicken Roll on Zucchini/Courgettes with Coffee Coriander Sauce

MAIN DISH

2 skinless, boneless chicken breasts,
5^1/$_2$-6^1/$_2$ oz/165-185 g each
10 stoned black olives, chopped
^{3}/$_4$ cup / 75 g / 3 oz sun-dried
tomatoes in oil, drained and chopped
1 bunch of fresh basil, finely chopped
4 tbsp grated pecorino cheese
^{3}/$_4$ cup / 200 ml / 7 fl oz chicken
stock
2 zucchini/courgettes, sliced
extra virgin olive oil
1 small red onion, cut into thin strips
sea salt
freshly ground black pepper
fresh basil sprigs, to garnish

Coffee coriander sauce:
^{3}/$_4$ cup / 200 ml / 7 fl oz chicken
stock
1 tbsp coriander seeds, crushed
1 tsp black peppercorns, crushed
1 tsp grated orange rind
1 tbsp ground coffee
1 shallot, finely chopped
1 tbsp diced celery
7 tbsp double cream
cayenne pepper

1 *Cut off and reserve the smaller fillets from the chicken breasts. Trim the larger pieces into neat rectangles. Sprinkle salt and pepper onto two sheets of tin foil and place a chicken rectangle on each.*

2 *Mix together the olives, sun-dried tomatoes, chopped basil and pecorino in a bowl and season with pepper. Spread this mixture evenly over the chicken rectangles. Put the smaller breast fillets in the middle. Using the tin foil, roll up the chicken rectangles securely. Fold over the tin foil tightly at both ends. Bring the chicken stock to the boil in a large pan, add the chicken rolls and cover. Switch off the heat and leave to stand on the stove for 20 minutes.*

3 *For the sauce, pour the chicken stock into a pan, add the coriander, peppercorns and orange rind, bring to the boil and simmer for 5 minutes over a medium heat. Spoon the coffee onto a square of muslin, tie securely and add to the pan with the shallot and celery. Simmer until the liquid has reduced by half. Stir in the cream, simmer until thickened. Season with salt and cayenne pepper.*

4 *Cut the zucchini/courgette slices into ^{1}/$_8$-in/3-mm thick batons. Place in a steamer and cook over a pan of boiling water for a few minutes, until tender. Tip into a bowl, season with sea salt and pepper and drizzle with olive oil. Add the red onion strips and toss lightly.*

5 *Remove the chicken rolls from the pan and unwrap, then cut into eight slices. Spoon some coffee coriander sauce on to serving plates and arrange the zucchini/courgettes on it. Then put the chicken roll slices on top. Garnish with basil.*

Lamb Fillet with Mocha Apple Sauce and Plantain Chips

14 oz / 400 g / 14 oz lamb fillet
1 plantain (green cooking banana)
olive or sunflower oil, for frying
4 baby egg-plants/aubergines, halved lengthways
16 pearl onions, peeled
7 tbsp dry white wine
fresh thyme, to garnish

Marinade:
1 tsp black peppercorns, crushed
1 tsp coriander seeds, crushed
1 tbsp fresh thyme leaves
2 tbsp extra virgin olive oil

Mocha apple sauce
3/4 cup / 200 ml / 7 fl oz apple juice
7 tbsp vegetable or chicken stock
1 tbsp Balsamic Mocha (see page 63)
1 tsp chili powder
1 shallot, finely chopped
15 coffee beans, ground
1/2 tsp fennel seeds
1 tsp curry powder
1/2 eating apple, unpeeled, cored and finely diced
pinch of freshly grated nutmeg
herbed sea salt

1 For the marinade, mix together the peppercorns, coriander, thyme and olive oil in a shallow dish. Add the lamb, turn to coat all over, cover and marinate for 1 hour in a cool place or overnight in the refrigerator.

2 Peel the plantain, halve crossways, then cut it lengthways into thin chips. Heat the olive or sunflower oil in a frying pan, add the plantain chips and fry until crisp. Remove with a slotted spoon and drain on kitchen paper.

3 For the mocha apple sauce, pour the apple juice and stock into a pan and add the balsamic mocha, chili powder, shallot, coffee, fennel seeds and curry powder. Bring to the boil and simmer until reduced to about 7 tbsp. Push the mixture through a fine sieve into a clean pan. Add the apple and bring back to the boil. Season with nutmeg and herbed salt to taste.

4 Heat a little more olive or sunflower oil in a frying pan, add the egg-plants/aubergines and pearl onions and cook over a medium heat until lightly golden and tender. Remove with a slotted spoon and drain on kitchen paper.

5 Add more oil to the pan, if necessary, and cook the lamb, turning occasionally, for about 8 minutes, until browned on the outside but still pink in the middle. Remove from the pan and drain on kitchen paper.

6 Pour the wine into the pan and bring to the boil to reduce slightly. Add the mocha apple sauce and bring to the boil. Toss the vegetables and lamb in the mixture. To serve, cut the lamb fillet into thick slices and arrange on serving plates with vegetables, fried plantain chips and remaining sauce.

Rabbit Saltimbocca on Stuffed Artichoke Hearts with Coffee Ginger Jus

MAIN DISH

4 rabbit fillets cut from the saddle
6 fresh sage leaves
1 fresh red chili, seeded and cut
into thin strips
6 slices Parma ham
extra virgin olive oil
1 bunch of rocket, leaves separated
freshly ground pepper

Stuffed artichoke hearts:
1 tbsp extra virgin olive oil
2 cups / 100 g / 3³/₄ oz
mushrooms, diced
8-10 spinach leaves, shredded
¹/₂ red pepper, peeled, seeded and
finely diced
7 tbsp double cream
1 small bunch of fresh flat parsley,
coarsely chopped
4 artichoke hearts

Coffee ginger jus:
1 tbsp castor sugar
7 tbsp freshly brewed strong coffee
1 shallot, finely chopped
¹/₄ cup / 50 g / 2 oz fresh root
ginger, cut into strips
¹/₄ cup / 50 ml / 2 fl oz beef
consommé
1 tsp acacia honey
1 tsp Balsamic Mocha (see page 63)
dash of soy sauce

1 Trim off any membrane from the rabbit fillets. Lay the sage leaves and chili strips on two of the fillets, place the remaining fillets on top and season with pepper. Wrap the Parma ham around both portions. Store in the refrigerator until you are ready to cook.

2 For the coffee ginger jus, heat the sugar in a heavy-based frying pan until it melts and turns golden brown. Pour in the coffee, add the shallot and ginger strips and bring to the boil. Cook until the mixture becomes syrupy. Add the consommé and heat again. Stir in the honey, balsamic mocha and soy sauce to taste.

3 For the artichoke stuffing, heat the oil in a heavy-based pan. Add the mushrooms and cook over a medium heat for a few minutes, then add the spinach strips and cook for a further 2-3 minutes. Stir in the red pepper and season well with pepper. Drain well into a clean pan, pressing out as much liquid as possible, and stir in the cream. Reserve the vegetables in the strainer. Bring the mixture to the boil and simmer until thickened. Stir in the vegetables and parsley.

4 Heat a little olive oil in a pan and fry the artichoke hearts until just tender. Stuff them with the mushroom mixture and keep warm.

5 Add more oil to the pan if necessary and fry the rabbit parcels over a medium heat for 5 minutes.

6 Arrange a bed of rocket on each serving plate and place the artichoke hearts on top. Cut the rabbit parcels in half diagonally and lay them on the stuffed artichoke hearts. Pour on the coffee ginger jus.

'Coffee is real good when you drink it; it gives you time to think. It's a lot more than just a drink; it's something happening. It gives you time... not actual hours or minutes, but a chance to be, like be yourself, and have a second cup.'

Gertrude Stein, US writer and critic (1874-1946)

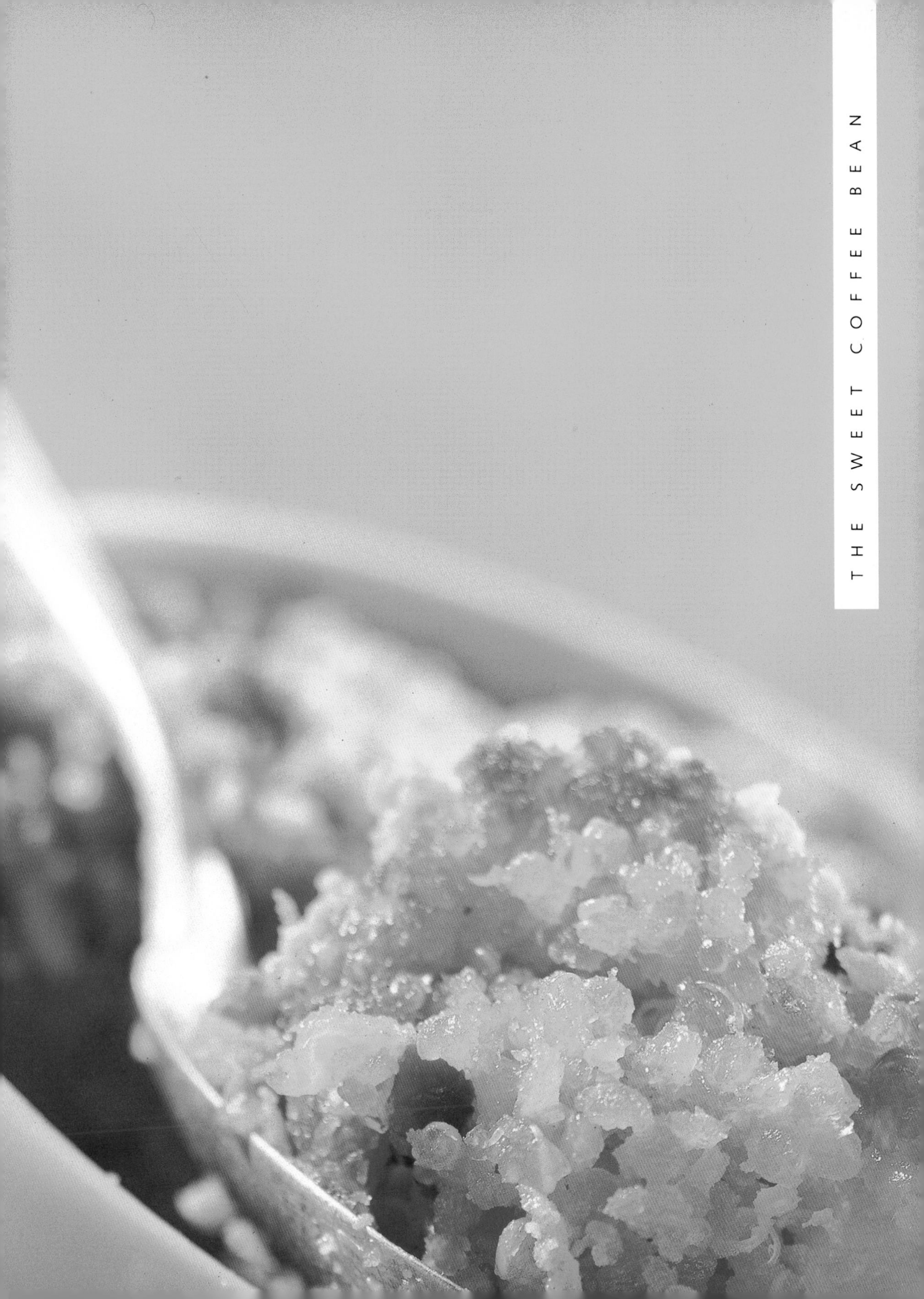

Quinoa Coffee Crumble

For 4 ovenproof china dishes:
contents 3/4 cup/180 ml/6 fl oz

Butter or margarine, for greasing
1/4 cup / 50 g / 2 oz quinoa
7 tbsp water
7 tbsp freshly brewed strong coffee
1/2 cinnamon stick
1/2 cup / 50 g / 2 oz dried pineapple
1/2 stick / 50 g / 2 oz butter
1 tbsp acacia honey
1 free-range egg, separated
1 tbsp castor sugar
50 orange segments
1 tsp ground cinnamon
sea salt

Crumble topping:
2 tbsp coarsely ground almonds
1 tbsp fresh white breadcrumbs
1 1/2 tsp butter or margarine
1 tsp ground cinnamon
1 tbsp soft dark brown sugar
1 tsp Sweet Coffee Essence (see page 56)

Preheat the oven to 180°C/350°F/Gas Mark 4.

1 Grease four 3/4-cup/180-ml/ 6 fl-oz ovenproof dishes with butter/margarine.

2 Put the quinoa, water, coffee, cinnamon stick, pineapple and a pinch of salt into a pan, bring to the boil and cook over a high heat for 2 minutes. Cover, turn off the heat and leave to stand on the stove for 20 minutes.

3 Mix all the crumble topping ingredients together in a bowl.

4 Beat together the butter and honey until light and fluffy, then stir in the egg yolk. Add the quinoa and mix gently.

5 Whisk the egg white stiff with a pinch of salt in a clean grease-free bowl. Add the sugar and beat until stiff. Fold the egg whites and orange segments into the quinoa mixture. Spoon the mixture into the prepared dishes and spread the crumble topping over it.

6 Bake for 20 minutes.

Tips:

Quinoa, pronounced keen-wha, is an ancient grain known to the Incas. It has recently become popular again and is a good source of protein and vitamins. It is also gluten free.

Serve with an apricot compote.

Peaches with Coffee Biscuit Filling

Butter or margarine, for greasing
4 ripe yellow peaches

Filling:
$1/2$ cup / 50 g / 2 oz plain
biscuits, such as petit beurre,
crushed
$1/2$ cup / 50 g / 2 oz walnuts,
coarsely chopped
1 tbsp coffee liqueur
1 tbsp double cream
1 tsp instant coffee powder
2 tsp grated orange rind

Meringue topping:
1 free-range egg white
pinch of sea salt
1 tbsp castor sugar

Preheat the oven to
200°C/400°F/Gas Mark 6.
1 Grease four $2^1/_2$-in/6-cm
tartlet tins.
2 For the filling, place all the
ingredients in a large bowl and
mix well.
3 Score the skins of the peaches
with a sharp knife, then blanch in
boiling water for about 1 minute.
Rinse under cold running water
and peel off the skins. Cut the
peaches lengthways without
slicing all the way through and
remove the stones.
4 For the meringue topping,
whisk the egg white with a pinch
of salt in a clean grease-free
bowl, then gradually whisk in the
sugar until stiff.

5 Place a peach in each of the
prepared tins. Fill them with the
biscuit mixture. Pile on the
meringue topping, making small
peaks.
6 Bake the filled peaches for
about 20 minutes. Keep an eye
on the meringue peaks to prevent
them from burning.

Tip:
Arrange in small bowls and serve
with iced vanilla sauce.

Coffee Mousse with...

3³/₄ oz / 100 g / 3³/₄ oz mocha
chocolate, finely chopped
2 tbsp milk
3 tbsp hot, freshly brewed
strong coffee
1 free-range egg white
pinch of sea salt
1 tsp castor sugar
³/₄ cup / 175 ml / 6 fl oz double
cream

1 *Place the chocolate in a bowl. Heat the milk to just below boiling point and pour it, together with the coffee, over the chocolate. Leave to stand for 2 minutes, then stir and leave to cool slightly.*
2 *Whip the egg white with the salt in a clean grease-free bowl until stiff, then gradually whisk in the sugar.*
3 *Whisk the cream in a separate bowl until stiff.*
4 *Fold the egg white, then the cream into the chocolate mixture. Cover with Saran wrap/clingfilm and chill for 2 hours.*
5 *To serve, sandwich scoops of the coffee mousse between tuiles (see opposite).*

Makes 20 biscuits

...Coffee Orange Tuiles*

1 stick / 100 g / 3³/₄ oz butter or margarine

2 oranges

10 coffee beans

¹/₂ cup / 50 g / 2 oz plain flour

¹/₂ cup / 100 g / 3³/₄ oz castor sugar

1 tablespoon instant coffee powder

⁵/₈ cup / 50 g / 2 oz flaked almonds

Preheat the oven to 180°C/350°F/Gas Mark 4.

1 *Line two baking sheets with non-stick wax/greaseproof paper.*

2 *Melt the butter in a small pan. Remove from the heat, leave to stand for a few minutes, then skim off the foam from the surface.*

3 *Remove the rind from the oranges using a citrus zester. Halve the fruits and squeeze out the juice. Strain the juice into a pan, add the coffee beans and heat until the liquid has reduced by half. Strain into a clean pan and heat again until reduced to about 3 tbsp.*

4 *Mix together butter, orange rind, orange juice, flour, sugar, instant coffee and almonds.*

5 *Line a baking tray with wax/greaseproof paper. Place spoonfuls of the mixture, spaced well apart, on the baking sheets. Press lightly with a fork to flatten to 3-in/7.5-cm rounds. You may need to do this in batches to allow plenty of room for expansion during baking.*

6 *Bake for 8 minutes. Leave the tuiles on the baking sheets for a few minutes to firm up slightly, then carefully transfer to wire racks to cool.*

* Tuiles are light cookies.

Coffee Parfait

2 free-range egg yolks

$^1/_8$ cup / 25 g / 1 oz castor sugar

1 tsp coffee liqueur

1 tsp Fruity Coffee Essence (see page 56)

1 free-range egg white

pinch of sea salt

$^2/_3$ cup / 150 ml / $^1/_4$ pint double cream

1 quantity Spicy Praline (see page 58), chopped

1 *Fold four sheets of wax/greaseproof paper into triple layered 10-cm/4-in wide strips. Wrap one strip around each of four coffee cups about 2 in/5 cm high and secure with an elastic band. Put them in the freezer.*

2 *Beat together the egg yolks, 1$^1/_2$ tsp of the sugar, the liqueur and coffee essence with a whisk or electric mixer until light and fluffy.*

3 *Whisk the egg white with the salt in a clean grease-free bowl until stiff. Gradually whisk in the remaining sugar.*

4 *Whisk the cream in another bowl until stiff.*

5 *Fold the egg white with half the praline into the egg yolk mixture, then fold in the cream. Divide the mixture among the chilled coffee cups and return them to the freezer for about 3 hours.*

6 *Ten minutes before serving, transfer the cups to the refrigerator. Remove and discard the paper collars, sprinkle the remaining praline on top of each parfait and serve immediately.*

Semolina Molds with Vanilla Coffee Sauce

Serves 4

1 vanilla pod
²/₃ cup / 150 ml / ¹/₄ pint milk
¹/₄ cup / 50 g / 2 oz castor sugar
¹/₂ tsp / 2.5 g / ¹/₈ oz sachet
agar-agar powder*
3 tbsp Fruity Coffee Essence (see
page 56)
pinch of sea salt
¹/₂ cup / 40 g / 1¹/₂ oz semolina
²/₃ cup / 150 ml / ¹/₄ pint
double cream
¹/₄ cup / 50 ml / 2 fl oz Sweet
Coffee Essence (see page 56)
1 Vanilla Mocha Cream
(see page 108)

Cherry compote:
2 tbsp castor sugar
¹/₄ cup / 50 ml / 2 fl oz red wine
¹/₂ cinnamon stick
1¹/₂ cups / 200 g / 7 oz
cherries, stoned

1 *Put four ¹/₂ cup-sized (120 ml/4 fl oz) molds into the freezer.*
2 *Slit the vanilla pod lengthways and scrape out the seeds. Pour the milk into a pan and add the vanilla pod and seeds, sugar, agar-agar powder and coffee essence. Bring to the boil, stirring constantly. Remove the pan from the heat and discard the vanilla pod. Gradually whisk the semolina into the milk mixture, adding it in a thin steady stream. Return the pan to the heat and simmer gently for 4 minutes. Pour the mixture into a bowl and stir until cold.*
3 *Whisk the cream in a separate bowl until stiff. Gently fold it into the semolina mixture before it begins to set. Spoon the mixture into the molds and chill in the refrigerator for 2-3 hours.*

4 *For the cherry compote put the sugar, wine and cinnamon in a pan and bring to the boil, stirring until the sugar has dissolved. Add the cherries and simmer over a low heat, without stirring, for 2 minutes. Strain the liquid into a clean pan and set over a high heat until reduced by half. Add the cherries and bring back to the boil. Remove from the heat, cover and leave to cool.*
5 *Carefully loosen the desserts from the edges of the molds and invert onto plates. Spoon the essence over them, add the vanilla mocha cream and serve with the cherry compote.*

*see recipe notes page 41.

Coffee Pannacotta with Kiwi Fruit, Pineapple and Praline

Serves 4

1³/₄ cups / 400 ml / 14 fl oz
double cream
20 coffee beans, ground
1 vanilla pod
2 tsp grated orange rind
¹/₂ tsp / 2.5 g / ¹/₈ oz sachet
agar-agar powder*
1 kiwi fruit
1 small pineapple
¹/₂ quantity Coffee Praline (see
page 58), chopped

1 *Pour 1¹/₃ cups/300 ml/¹/₂ pint of the cream into a pan, add the coffee and bring to the boil. Remove the pan from the heat, cover and leave to stand for 30 minutes. Strain into a clean pan.*
2 *Slit the vanilla pod lengthways and scrape out the seeds. Add the vanilla pod and seeds, orange rind, agar-agar powder and remaining cream to the pan and bring to the boil, stirring until the mixture is smooth. Remove the vanilla pod and pour the mixture into four ¹/₂ cup-sized (120 ml/4 fl oz) molds. Leave to cool at room temperature, then chill in the refrigerator for 2-3 hours.*
3 *Peel and dice the kiwi fruit. Peel the pineapple, cut out the 'eyes' and cut the fruit in half. Remove and discard the core, then cut the flesh into dice.*
4 *Briefly dip the base of the molds in hot water, carefully loosen around the edges and invert on to plates. Decorate with kiwi and pineapple dice and chopped coffee praline.*

*see recipe notes page 41.

Tricolor Mocha Cream

Chocolate cream:

5 oz / 150 g / 5 oz plain chocolate, finely chopped

3/4 cup / 200 ml / 7 fl oz milk

1 cinnamon stick

1/4 cup / 50 g / 2 oz castor sugar

1 1/2 tsp cornstarch/cornflour

1/4 cup / 50 ml / 2 fl oz double cream

1 tbsp brandy

Coffee cream:

1 cup / 200 ml / 7 fl oz double cream

3 tbsp Sweet Coffee Essence (see page 56)

1 tbsp instant coffee powder

1 free-range egg yolk

1 free-range egg

1/4 cup / 50 g / 2 oz soft dark brown sugar

Vanilla mocha cream:

1 vanilla pod

3/4 cup / 200 ml / 7 fl oz milk

2 tsp grated orange rind

1/4 cup / 50 g / 2 oz coffee beans, ground

1/8 cup / 25 g / 1 oz vanilla sugar

2 tsp / 10 g / 1/2 oz cornstarch/ cornflour

2 egg yolks

1/4 cup / 50 g / 2 oz castor sugar

7 tbsp double cream

1 For the chocolate cream, place the chocolate in a bowl. Pour 2/3 cup/150 ml/1/4 pint of the milk into a pan, add the cinnamon stick and bring to the boil. Remove from the heat and pour over the chocolate. Mix together the remaining milk, sugar and cornstarch in a small bowl. Pour the chocolate milk into a pan and bring to the boil. Add the milk mixture and bring back to the boil, stirring constantly. Strain into a bowl, cover with Saran wrap/clingfilm, leave to cool at room temperature, then chill in the refrigerator for 2 hours.

2 For the coffee cream, pour 2/3 cup/150 ml/1/4 pint of the cream into a pan, add the coffee essence and the instant coffee powder and bring to the boil. Strain the mixture into a jug. Beat together the egg yolk, egg and brown sugar in a heatproof bowl until light and fluffy. Gradually beat in the coffee cream. Set the bowl over a pan of simmering water and whisk until foamy. Remove from the heat, place in a bowl of iced water and whisk until cold.

3 For the vanilla cream, slit the vanilla pod lengthways and scrape out the seeds. Pour 2/3 cup/150 ml/1/4 pint of the milk into a pan, add the vanilla pod and seeds and

orange rind and bring to the boil. Place the coffee in a bowl, pour over the milk mixture and leave to stand for 20 minutes. Mix together the remaining milk, vanilla sugar and cornflour in a small bowl. Beat together the egg yolk and sugar until light and fluffy and stir into the vanilla milk. Strain the coffee milk through into a pan and bring to the boil. Stir it into the egg yolk mixture, return to the pan and bring to just below boiling point, stirring constantly. Pour the mixture into a bowl, cover with Saran wrap/clingfilm, leave to cool at room temperature, then chill in the refrigerator for 2 hours.

4 Stir the chocolate cream until smooth. Whisk the double cream until stiff, fold it into the chocolate cream and add the brandy.

5 Stir the coffee cream until smooth. Whisk the remaining double cream and fold it into the coffee cream.

6 Stir the vanilla mocha cream until smooth. Whisk the double cream until stiff and fold it into the vanilla cream.

7 Put chocolate, coffee and vanilla creams into separate piping bags, fitted with a large plain nozzle and pipe them into glasses one layer at a time. You can decorate the desserts with more cream if you like.

Pale Spicy Coffee Mousse with...

1 cup / 250 ml / 9 fl oz freshly brewed strong coffee
1 vanilla pod, slit lengthways
1 clove
1/2 stick cinnamon
1 bay leaf
15 coriander seeds, crushed
1 x 1/4 oz/5 g sachet agar-agar powder*
3 oz / 75 g / 3 oz good-quality white chocolate, finely chopped
2 free-range egg yolks
1 teaspoon coffee liqueur
1 teaspoon brandy
3/4 cup / 175 ml / 6 fl oz double cream
1 free-range egg white
pinch of sea salt
1 tsp sugar
4 tbsp chopped Spicy Praline (see page 58), to decorate

*see recipe notes page 41.

1 Pour the coffee into a pan, add the vanilla pod, clove, cinnamon, bay leaf, coriander seeds and agar-agar powder and bring to the boil. Simmer over a medium heat until reduced to about 6 tbsp. Strain into a bowl and leave to cool.

2 Melt the chocolate in a heatproof bowl set over a pan of barely simmering water. Remove the bowl from the heat.

3 Beat together the egg yolk, liqueur and brandy in another heatproof bowl set over a pan of simmering water until thickened and pale. Remove the bowl from the heat and stir in the coffee mixture and the melted chocolate.

4 Whisk the egg white with a pinch of salt in a clean grease-free bowl until stiff. Gradually whisk in the sugar, then fold it into the mousse. Whisk the cream until stiff and fold it into the mousse. Cover the bowl with Saran wrap/clingfilm and chill in the refrigerator for 3 hours.

...Layer Cake

2¹/₂ oz / 65 g / 2¹/₂ oz butter, softened

1¹/₂ oz / 40 g / 1¹/₂ oz marzipan, grated

grated rind of 1 lemon

¹/₂ vanilla pod

3 free-range eggs, separated

¹/₃ cup / 65 g / 2¹/₂ oz castor sugar

1 tbsp single cream

¹/₄ cup / 25 g / 1 oz plain flour

¹/₃ cup / 40 g / 1¹/₂ oz cornstarch/cornflour

pinch of sea salt

Preheat the oven to 220°C/425°F/Gas Mark 7.

1 Line the base of a 5-in/12-cm loose-based cake tin with wax/greaseproof paper.

2 Beat together the butter and marzipan until light and smooth, then stir in the lemon rind.

3 Scrape out the seeds from the vanilla pod and add the seeds to the egg yolks with half the sugar. Beat well until pale and fluffy. Stir in the cream. Add the butter and marzipan mixture and beat until smooth. Sift together the flour, cornstarch and salt and fold them into the mixture.

4 Whisk the egg whites in a clean grease-free bowl until softly peaking, then gradually whisk in the remaining sugar until stiff. Gently fold the egg whites into the cake batter.

5 Spoon the batter into a disposable icing bag and snip off the tip. Pipe the first layer ¹/₈ in/3 mm deep onto the base of the cake tin. Put it on the bottom rack of the oven and bake until golden brown. Remove the tin from the oven and pipe in the next layer. Continue in this way until all the mixture is used up.

6 Leave the cake to cool.

Serving

Form the mousse into small balls with a cold tablespoon and arrange on plates. Cut the cake into thin slices and arrange on the plate. Decorate with spicy praline.

Coffee Pancake with Pears in Spicy Syrup

Coffee pancake:

$^1/_4$ cup / 50 ml / 2 fl oz double cream

10 coffee beans, ground

1 tsp Fruity Coffee Essence (see page 56)

2 free-range eggs, separated

pinch of vanilla sugar

2 tsp grated orange rind

1 tsp rum

$^1/_4$ cup / 25 g / 1 oz plain flour

2 tbsp castor sugar

pinch of sea salt

clarified butter for frying

$^1/_2$ oz / 15 g / $^1/_2$ oz butter or margarine

icing sugar, for sprinkling

Pear compote:

2 Williams pears, peeled, halved and cored

1 cinnamon stick

1 tbsp castor sugar

1 quantity Mexican Spicy Syrup (see page 60)

juice of $^1/_2$ lemon

1 *For the compote, slice the pears. Pour 2 cups/500 ml/18 fl oz water into a pan, add the cinnamon stick and sugar and bring to the boil, stirring until the sugar has dissolved. Add the pear slices and poach over a low heat for 5 minutes. Drain, reserving the syrup. Bring the syrup back to the boil, add the pear slices with the lemon juice and bring to the boil again. Remove the pan from the heat, cover and leave to cool.*

2 *Preheat the oven to 180°C/350°F/Gas Mark 4.*

3 *For the pancake, heat the cream to just below boiling point, then pour it over the coffee in a bowl. Cover with Saran wrap/clingfilm, leave to cool, then chill in the refrigerator. Strain the coffee cream into another bowl, add the fruity coffee essence, egg yolks, vanilla sugar, orange rind, rum and flour and stir to a smooth batter. Whisk the egg whites with a pinch of salt in a clean grease-free bowl until softly peaking. Gradually whisk in the sugar and until stiff. Fold the egg whites into the batter.*

4 *Melt the clarified butter in a warmed ovenproof dish or pan and add the batter. Bake for about 10 minutes, until the top is golden brown. Cut the pancake into diamond shapes. Add the butter/margarine and briefly bake again. Sprinkle with icing sugar and caramelize under a preheated grill.*

5 *Arrange the pancake with the pears and decorate with the spicy syrup.*

Variation

A fruit sauce made from apricots, damsons or cherries also goes well with the coffee pancake.

'Coffee, which makes the politician wise

And see through all things with his

half-shut eyes.'

Alexander Pope, English poet and writer (1688-1744)

Brioches Filled with Coffee-marinated Fruit

Makes 8

Filling:
1/2 cup / 75 g / 3 oz mixed dried fruit, finely diced
1/4 cup / 50 ml / 2 fl oz freshly brewed strong coffee
1 tbsp brandy
1 tsp castor sugar

Brioche dough:
2/3 cup / 150 ml / 1/4 pint milk
1/8 cup / 20 g / 3/4 oz castor sugar
1/8 cup / 20 g / 1/4 oz dried yeast
41/2 cups / 500 g / 11/4 lb plain flour
1 free-range egg
4 large egg yolks
11/2 tsp salt
3/4 cup / 165 g / 51/2 oz butter or margarine, softened, plus extra for greasing
lightly beaten egg yolk, to glaze

1 *For the dried fruit filling, mix all the ingredients together in a bowl and marinate for 2 hours.*

2 *For the dough, heat 1/4 cup/50 ml/2 fl oz of the milk until it is just lukewarm. Pour it into a bowl and stir in the sugar, yeast and 1/4 cup/20 g/3/4 oz of the flour, cover with Saran wrap/clingfilm and set aside to rise in a warm place for 40 minutes, until it has doubled in volume.*

3 *Stir the remaining milk, the egg and egg yolks into the dough. Sift in the flour and salt and knead to a firm dough. Dot the dough with butter and knead in. Place it in a food processor, fitted with dough hooks, and process at medium speed for 20 minutes. Turn into a bowl, cover with Saran wrap/clingfilm and set aside in a warm place to rise for 30 minutes.*

4 *Squeeze out the dried fruit and knead together with 4 oz/115 g/4 oz of the brioche dough.*

5 *Preheat the oven to 220°C/425°C/Gas Mark 7. Grease eight individual brioche tins with butter/margarine.*

6 *Knead the dough thoroughly. Set aside about 7 oz/200 g/7 oz of it for the 'tops'. Divide the remaining dough into eight equal portions and form these into 21/2-in/6-cm rounds. Divide the fruit filling among the rounds, placing it in the middle of each. Form the rounds into balls and put them into the prepared tins. Brush with beaten egg yolk. Make eight small balls from the reserved dough and place one on top of each of the larger balls. Brush with beaten egg yolk.*

7 *Place the tins on the middle rack of the oven. Pour about 1/4 cup/50 ml/2 fl oz water onto the oven floor and shut the door immediately so that the steam cannot escape. Lower the oven temperature to 180°C/350°F/Gas Mark 4. Bake the brioches for 10 minutes.*

Coffee Buñuelos (Fritters)

1/2 cup / 120 ml / 4 fl oz water
1 teaspoon orange liqueur
5 coffee beans, ground
2 tsp grated orange rind
2 1/4 cups / 250 g / 9 oz plain flour, plus extra for dusting
pinch of sea salt
1 free-range egg yolk
1 tbsp castor sugar
1 tbsp / 15 g / 1/2 oz butter, chilled and diced
2 cups / 500 ml / 18 fl oz groundnut oil, for deep-frying
icing sugar, for dusting

1 *Pour the water and liqueur into a pan, add the coffee and orange rind and bring to the boil. Strain into a bowl, leave to cool, then chill in the refrigerator.*
2 *Sift the flour into a bowl and make a well in the center. Put the salt, egg yolk, sugar and diced butter into the hollow. Gradually incorporate the flour with your fingertips until the mixture resembles breadcrumbs. Add the chilled liquid, a spoonful at a time, and mix together to form an elastic dough. Leave to rest for about 20 minutes.*
3 *Divide the dough into 12 portions. Form these into balls and roll them in a little flour to dust lightly. Flatten the balls with your hand until they are about 6 in/15 cm in diameter.*
4 *Heat the oil in a deep frying pan to 180°C/350°F or until a cube of day-old bread browns in about 45 seconds. Fry the buñuelos, one at a time, until golden brown.*
5 *Drain on kitchen paper and dust with icing sugar while they are still warm.*

Tip:
These Mexican fritters are good served with Mexican Spicy Coffee (see page 50).

Coffee Doughnuts

1/2 cup / 120 ml / 4 fl oz milk
1 tbsp instant coffee powder
pinch of sea salt
2 tsp grated orange rind
1 tsp grated fresh root ginger
1 1/2 oz / 40 g / 1 1/2 oz butter
2/3 cup / 75 g / 3 oz plain flour
2 free-range eggs
2 cups / 500 ml / 18 fl oz
groundnut oil, for deep-frying
cinnamon sugar, for dusting

1 *Pour the milk into a pan, add the instant coffee, salt, orange rind, ginger and butter and bring to the boil. Pour in the flour, turn off the heat and stir the mixture on the stove until it comes away from the base of the pan. Leave to cool.*
2 *Beat the eggs and gradually fold them into the dough.*
3 *Heat the oil in a deep frying pan to 180°C/350°F or until a cube of day-old bread browns in about 45 seconds.*
4 *Form the dough into small balls with a teaspoon. Fry them, in batches, until golden brown. Drain on kitchen paper, then roll the doughnuts in cinnamon sugar.*

T i p s :
Make cinnamon sugar by mixing equal quantities of castor sugar and ground cinnamon.
Serve with a vanilla or fruit sauce.

Fritters with Coffee Ricotta Filling

Makes 12

Filling:
¹/₄ cup / 115 g / 4 oz ricotta cheese
1 tbsp lemon juice
¹/₃ cup / 50 g / 2 oz almonds, coarsely ground
1 tbsp Fruity Coffee Essence (see page 56)
grated rind of ¹/₂ orange
¹/₄ cup / 20 g / ³/₄ oz sultanas
1 tbsp double cream

Dough:
1¹/₃ cup / 150 g / 5 oz plain flour
1 tbsp / 25 g / 1 oz butter or margarine, softened and diced
1 free-range egg
1 tbsp castor sugar
pinch of sea salt
grated rind of 1 orange
1 tsp Sweet Coffee Essence (see page 56)
1 tbsp milk
1 egg white, lightly beaten
groundnut oil, for frying
cinnamon sugar, for dusting

Variation
Omit the almonds, Fruity Coffee Essence and sultanas from the filling and substitute grated Parmesan cheese, chopped and seeded fresh chili and a little Mexican Spice Paste (see page 58) instead. Serve with pre-dinner drinks.

1 *For the filling, mix all the ingredients together in a bowl and chill in the refrigerator for 1 hour.*
2 *For the dough, sift the flour into a bowl and make a well in the center. Dot the butter over the flour. Lightly beat together the egg, sugar, salt, orange rind, coffee essence and milk and pour into the well. Gradually incorporate the flour and knead to a firm dough. Wrap it in Saran wrap/clingfilm and leave it to rest for 1 hour.*
3 *Roll out the dough and divide it into 12 portions. Then roll each portion into a 3-in/7.5-cm round. Divide the filling among the rounds, placing it in the middle of each. Brush the edges with egg white and fold over to make little turnovers. Decorate the edges (see photo, page 45).*
4 *Heat the oil in a deep-fryer to 200°C/400°F or until a cube of day-old bread browns in 30 seconds. Fry the fritters, in batches if necessary, until golden brown. Drain on kitchen paper, dust with cinnamon sugar and serve while they are still warm.*

Light Mocha Sponge

1¹/₂ / 40 g / 1¹/₂ oz butter or
margarine, plus extra for
greasing
plain flour, for dusting
1 oz / 25 g / 1 oz plain
chocolate, chopped
¹/₄ cup / 50 ml / 2 fl oz Sweet
Coffee Essence (see page 56)
2 tsp grated orange rind
1¹/₂ oz / 40 g / 1¹/₂ oz marzipan
1 free-range egg
3 free-range egg yolks
¹/₂ cup / 90 g / 3¹/₂ oz castor
sugar
2 tbsp cocoa powder
1 tbsp instant coffee powder
2 free-range egg whites
pinch of sea salt
3 tbsp drinking chocolate
powder

*Preheat the oven to
180°C/350°F/Gas Mark 4.*
1 *Grease the base and sides of a
9-10 in/23-25 cm springform*
cake tin with butter. Dust with
flour.*
2 *Melt the chocolate in a
heatproof bowl set over a pan of
barely simmering water. Remove
from the heat and stir in the
coffee essence, butter/margarine
and orange rind. Work in the
marzipan until it is fully
incorporated.*
3 *Beat the egg and egg yolks
with ³/₈ cup/75 g/3 oz sugar, 1
tbsp of the cocoa powder and the
instant coffee, until the sugar has
dissolved and the mixture is
fluffy. Fold into the chocolate
mixture.*
4 *Whisk the egg whites with the
salt in a clean grease-free bowl
until softly peaking. Gradually
whisk in the remaining sugar
until stiff. Carefully fold the egg
whites into the chocolate
mixture, then spoon into the
prepared tin.*
5 *Bake for about 30 minutes.
Place the cake tin on a plate
covered with a dish towel and
leave to cool.*

6 *Sift together the drinking
chocolate and remaining cocoa
powder. Remove the cake tin and
sprinkle the sponge with the
chocolate and cocoa mixture.*

Tip:
*Flavor fluffy whipped cream with
vanilla sugar and serve with the
sponge.*

**Springform cake tin – one with
a spring clasp/release.*

Coffee Gugelhupf
(Buttery Coffee Cake)

Butter or margarine, for greasing
fresh white breadcrumbs, for
sprinkling
2 tbsp rum
$^{1}/_{4}$ cup / 40 g / 1$^{1}/_{2}$ oz raisins
$^{1}/_{3}$ cup / 50 g / 2 oz grated tart
apple
$^{1}/_{4}$ cup / 40 g / 1$^{1}/_{2}$ oz almonds,
coarsely ground
grated rind of $^{1}/_{2}$ orange
$^{7}/_{8}$ cup / 100 g / 3$^{3}/_{4}$ oz plain
flour
$^{1}/_{2}$ cup / 65 g / 2$^{1}/_{2}$ oz
cornstarch/cornflour
1 tsp baking powder
3 free-range eggs
$^{3}/_{8}$ cup / 75 g / 3 oz castor sugar
$^{1}/_{4}$ cup / 50 ml / 2 fl oz Sweet
Coffee Essence (see page 56)
1 vanilla pod, slit lengthways
$^{3}/_{4}$ cup / 175 g / 6 oz butter,
melted
icing sugar, for dusting

*Preheat the oven to
180°C/350°F/Gas Mark 4.*

*1 Grease a 1 quart/1 liter/1$^{3}/_{4}$
pint gugelhupf tin or ring mold
with butter/margarine and
sprinkle it with breadcrumbs.*

*2 Gently heat the rum, then add
the raisins and set aside to soak.
Mix together the apple, almonds
and orange rind. Sift together the
flour, cornstarch and baking
powder into another bowl.*

*3 Beat together the eggs and
sugar in a heatproof bowl over a
pan of barely simmering water
for 2 minutes. Remove from the
heat. Add the coffee essence,
scrape out the vanilla seeds into
the bowl and briefly beat again.
Fold in the apple and almond
mixture, then fold in the flour
mixture. Mix the melted butter
with 4 tbsp of the dough and
gently stir it into the mixture.
Add the raisins. Spoon the dough
into the prepared cake tin or
mold.*

*4 Bake for 45 minutes. Turn
out the cake on to a wire rack,
dust with icing sugar and leave
it to cool.*

Coffee Fruit Cake

Butter or margarine, for greasing
1 cup / 100 g / 3³/₄ oz currants
1 tbsp kirsch
1¹/₈ cups / 250 g / 9 oz butter
1¹/₂ cups / 300 g / 11 oz castor
sugar
8 free-range eggs
1¹/₃ cups / 250 g / 9 oz plain
flour
1 tsp baking powder
pinch of sea salt

Light mixture:
¹/₃ cup / 50 g / 2 oz soaked
raisins
2 tbsp instant coffee powder

Dark mixture:
¹/₈ cup / 20 g / 3/4 oz cocoa
powder
¹/₄ cup / 50 ml / 2 fl oz Sweet
Coffee Essence (see page 56)
1 cup / 150 g / 5 oz candied
fruits

For the glaze:
1 tbsp kirsch
1 tbsp pear juice

Preheat the oven to 220°C/425°F/Gas Mark 7.

1 Grease a 10-in/25-cm long loaf tin and line it with wax/greaseproof paper.

2 Place the currants in a bowl, add the kirsch and set aside to soak.

3 Cream the butter/margarine with 1¹/₄ cups/250 g/9 oz of the sugar. Separate six of the eggs, then add the remaining whole eggs to the bowl of egg yolks and mix together. Gradually add the egg mixture, one spoonful at a time, into the butter mixture. Sift together the flour and baking powder and gently fold in.

4 Put half the mixture into another bowl. For the light mixture, stir the raisins and the coffee powder into one portion. For the dark mixture, stir the cocoa powder, coffee essence and candied fruits into the second portion.

5 Whisk the egg whites with the salt in a clean grease-free bowl until softly peaking. Gradually whisk in the remaining sugar until stiff. Fold half the egg whites into each mixture.

6 Spoon the dark mixture into the prepared tin. Spoon the light mixture into a piping bag fitted with a large plain nozzle. Press the nozzle into the dark mixture and gently squeeze the bag to distribute the light mixture evenly.

7 Bake for 10 minutes, then lower the oven temperature to 180°C/350°F/Gas Mark 4 and bake for a further 50 minutes. Halfway through the cooking time, check the cake and if the top is browning too quickly, cover it with tin foil.

8 Turn out the cake onto a wire rack. Mix together the kirsch and pear juice and brush all over the cake while it is still warm.

Coffee Tarts

Makes 2 x 4¹/₂-in/12-cm tarts

Pastry:
³/₈ cup / 90 g / 3¹/₂ oz butter,
softened, or margarine, plus
extra for greasing
¹/₃ cup / 40 g / 1¹/₂ oz icing
sugar
1 free-range egg yolk
1¹/₄ cups / 150 g / 5 oz plain
flour, plus extra for dusting
pinch of sea salt

Filling:
¹/₂ stick / 50 g / 2 oz butter,
softened
¹/₂ cup / 90 g / 3¹/₂ oz castor
sugar
3 free-range eggs
2 tbsp freshly brewed strong
coffee, cooled
1 tbsp coffee liqueur
1 tbsp orange liqueur
grated rind of 1 orange

1 *Mix together the butter, icing sugar and egg yolk until smooth and creamy. Sift in the flour and salt and knead gently to a firm dough. Form into a roll, cover with Saran wrap/clingfilm and leave to rest in the refrigerator for 1 hour.*

2 *Preheat the oven to 180°C/350°F/Gas Mark 4. Grease and flour two 4¹/₂-in/12-cm tart tins.*

3 *Divide the dough in half, roll out each portion and use to line the prepared tins. Then line the pastry cases with wax/greaseproof paper and fill with baking beans. Bake for 15 minutes. Remove the pastry cases, but leave the oven on. Remove the beans and paper.*

4 *For the filling, beat together the butter/margarine and sugar until pale and fluffy, then beat in the eggs, one at a time. Gradually beat in the remaining ingredients. Spoon the filling evenly over the pastry cases.*

5 *Bake for about 20 minutes.*

Mocha Pear Cake

Serves 12

4 bottled William pears

2 tbsp pear brandy

2 tbsp pear juice

Dark filling:

7 oz / 200 g / 7 oz plain chocolate, finely chopped

2 tsp grated orange rind

1 cup / 200 ml / 7 fl oz double cream

1 tsp Sweet Coffee Essence (see page 56)

Light filling:

7 oz / 200 g / 7 oz milk chocolate, finely chopped

1 tsp finely grated fresh root ginger

1 cup / 200 ml / 7 fl oz double cream

1 vanilla pod, slit lengthways

$^1/_2$ tsp agar-agar powder*

Icing:

12 oz / 350 g / 12 oz plain chocolate, finely chopped

$^3/_4$ /cup / 200 ml / 7 fl oz milk

2 tbsp / 25 ml / 1 fl oz pear juice

2 tbsp / 25 g / 1 oz butter, softened

*see recipe notes page 41.

Sponge:

4 free-range eggs, separated

$^5/_8$ cup / 115 g / 4 oz castor sugar

$^7/_8$ cup / 100 g / $3^3/_4$ oz plain flour

2 tbsp instant coffee powder

pinch of salt

1 Slice the pears and pat dry on kitchen paper. Mix together the brandy and pear juice.

2 For the dark filling, mix together the chocolate and orange rind. Bring $^2/_3$ cup/150 ml/$^1/_4$ pint of the cream to the boil, then pour over the chocolate. Leave to stand for 2 minutes. Add the coffee essence, mix well and leave to cool. Whisk the remaining cream until stiff and fold it in.

3 For the light filling, mix together the chocolate and ginger. Pour $^2/_3$ cup/150 ml/$^1/_4$ pint of the cream into a pan. Scrape out the vanilla seeds into the pan, add the agar-agar powder and bring to the boil, stirring constantly. Pour over the chocolate and leave to stand for 2 minutes. Mix well and leave it

to cool. Whisk the remaining cream until stiff and fold it in.

4 For the icing, put the chocolate in a bowl. Bring the milk to just below boiling point, pour over the chocolate and stir gently until the chocolate has melted. Stir in the pear juice and butter and mix to a smooth, shiny icing.

5 Line a Swiss Roll tin with wax/greaseproof paper. Preheat the oven to 180°C/350°F/Gas Mark 4.

6 For the sponge, beat the egg yolks with $^1/_2$ cup/100 g/$3^3/_4$ oz of the sugar until pale and fluffy. Sift together the flour and coffee powder and fold into the egg yolk mixture. Whisk the egg whites with the salt in a clean grease-free bowl until softly peaking. Gradually whisk in the remaining sugar until stiff. Gently fold the egg whites into the egg yolk mixture. Spoon the mixture into the prepared tin. Bake for 8 minutes. Turn out the sponge onto a dish towel, peel off the wax/greaseproof paper, then lay it back on top of the sponge and leave to cool.

Continued on page 132

Coffee Amaretti (Crisp Almond Cookies)

1³/₄ cups / 300 g / 11 oz almonds, coarsely ground
¹/₂ cup / 100 g / 3³/₄ oz castor sugar
6 tbsp free-range egg white
1 tbsp almond extract
⁷/₈ cup / 100 g / 3³/₄ oz icing sugar
2 tbsp Sweet Coffee Essence (see page 56)

1 Line a baking sheet with wax/greaseproof paper.
2 Place the almonds, sugar, half the egg white and almond extract in a bowl and rub together until the mixture resembles marzipan.
3 Whisk the remaining egg white with the icing sugar in a clean grease-free bowl until softly peaking. Fold into the almond mixture, together with the coffee essence.
4 Spoon the mixture into a piping bag fitted with a plain nozzle. Pipe walnut-size semi-circles onto the prepared baking sheet. Cover with a dish towel and leave to dry out for 10-12 hours. Press the edges inwards.
5 Preheat the oven to 230°C/450°F/Gas Mark 8. Bake the amaretti for about 5 minutes. Cool on a wire rack.

Continued from page 131

7 Cut the sponge into three equal rectangles and sprinkle with the brandy and pear juice mixture.
8 Spread two-thirds of the dark filling evenly over one rectangle. Spread all the light filling evenly over the second rectangle. Chill in the refrigerator for 5 minutes. Arrange the pear slices on top of each coated sponge rectangle. Using a spatula, lay the rectangle with the light filling on top of the one with the dark filling. Top with the third rectangle. Spread the remaining dark filling over the top rectangle. Chill in the refrigerator for at least 1 hour.
9 Spread the lukewarm chocolate icing over the top and sides of the cake.
10 Leave the cake overnight in the refrigerator before serving.

Mocha Macaroons

Makes 10

¹/₂ cup / 75 g / 3 oz almonds, finely ground
2 tsp / 10 g / ¹/₄ oz instant coffee powder
¹/₂ cup / 175 g / 6 oz icing sugar
5 tbsp free-range egg whites
pinch of salt

Mocha filling:
3³/₄ oz / 100 g / 3³/₄ oz plain chocolate, finely chopped
2 tbsp milk
3 tbsp freshly brewed strong coffee
¹/₄ cup / 50 ml / 2 fl oz double cream, stiffly whipped

Preheat the oven to 180°C/350°F/Gas Mark 4.
1 *Line two baking sheets with wax/greaseproof paper.*
2 *Mix together the almonds, coffee powder and ¹/₂ cup/ 100 g/3³/₄ oz of the icing sugar. Whisk the egg whites stiff with the salt in a clean grease-free bowl until softly peaking. Gradually whisk in the remaining icing sugar until stiff.*
3 *Gently fold the egg whites into the almond mixture. Spoon the mixture into a disposable icing bag. Snip off the tip to make a ¹/₄-in/5-mm opening. Pipe 20 rounds with a 1-in/2.5-cm diameter onto the prepared baking sheets.*
4 *Bake for 20 minutes, then carefully transfer to a wire rack to cool.*

5 *For the filling, place the chocolate in a bowl. Heat the milk to just below boiling point and pour it over the chocolate, together with the coffee. Leave to stand for 2 minutes, stir well and leave to cool. Fold in the whipped cream.*
6 *Spread the filling onto the flat side of 10 macaroons and place another macaroon on top of each.*
7 *Store the macaroons in an airtight container in a cool place for 1 day before serving.*

FAIR-TRADE COFFEE

Fair-trade coffee and other ingredients are now widely available in North America, Europe and Australasia. If you can't find them in the place where you normally shop, please ask for them: this is an important way to promote fair trade. The brand name may vary from country to country, but a single trademark is increasingly used for certification. It looks like this:

If the pack carries this trademark, you can be sure the contents meet the criteria laid down by the **Fairtrade Labelling Organization (FLO)**. Check out the criteria, and which brands have been awarded the trademark in your country, on their website
www.fairtrade.net

The International Federation for Alternative Trade (IFAT)
This is a network of fair-trade organizations in 47 countries, many of them Southern producers. They have agreed common objectives:

> To improve the livelihoods of producers
>
> To promote development opportunities for disadvantaged producers
>
> To raise consumer awareness
>
> To set an example of partnership in trade
>
> To campaign for changes in conventional trade
>
> To protect human rights

www.ifat.org

 NEW INTERNATIONALIST PUBLICATIONS
An independent co-operative based in Oxford, with offices in Adelaide, Christchurch, Dublin and Toronto, we exist 'to report on the people, the ideas, the action in the fight for global justice'.

As well as the monthly *New Internationalist* magazine and the English-language edition of *The World Guide*, we publish the *No-Nonsense Guides* and a series of best-selling cookbooks including *Quick & Easy – Vegetarian recipes from around the world for Western kitchens*. These, together with a range of other publications and products, can be purchased directly through our website, which features a major archive of related material.
www.newint.org